The Digital Tsunami

The Digital Tsunami

The Innovators Dilemma of the Modern
Media Industry or How Data-Driven
Advertising Turns the Media Market
Upside Down

by

Nicolas Clasen

Proofreading by Max Edwards

ISBN-13: 978-1492968979
ISBN-10: 1492968978

Table of Contents

CHAPTER ONE: DIGITAL TSUNAMI OR MEAN HIGH WATER? 13
Digitization as driver of innovation 14
Attack from the net 16
   Apple dominates the market for digital paid content 16
   Amazon morphs into a digital distribution platform 17
The shift of the branding budgets 18
Media managers are optimistic about the future 20

CHAPTER TWO: CHRISTENSEN'S MODEL OF DISRUPTIVE INNOVATIONS 25
Disruptive innovations create their own markets 26
Prisoners of their own customers 27
What goes up can't go down 27
Also business models are technologies 29

CHAPTER THREE: THE INNOVATOR'S DILEMMA OF THE TRADITIONAL MEDIA COMPANIES 30
The return channel as disruptive basis innovation 31
   Inclusion of users reaction in real time 32
The transfer of the established models 34
   The move away from the click 35
   The emergence of ad networks and arbitrage 36
The reach paradigm 37

CHAPTER FOUR: DATA-DRIVEN ADVERTISING AS A DISRUPTIVE INNOVATION 38
The Google model 39
   The grandsons of Adam Smith 40
   The search as a pre-filter for interested buyers 40
   Data to increase advertising relevance 41
   Google educates its advertisers 42

Google advertising and the AIDA model **43**
  Digression: The AIDA model 43
  Ad spending per usage time unit..44
  Search engine marketing as a direct sales tool.........................46
The technological s-curve **47**
  Real-time bidding: The Google model into a thousand pieces....47
  Strategic positioning within the real-time advertising market....48
  The ad exchange model..49
  Supply-side and demand-side platforms 51
  From key word to user targeting 52
Facebook: Exhibitionism as part of the system **53**
  The self-defining target group 54
  Campaign optimization based on the user reaction in real time.54
  Social targeting as a new dimension...55
  Facebook copies the Google ad system.....................................55
The technology jump **58**
  Real-time bidding threatened Google's core business 59

CHAPTER FIVE: THE BRANDING BET **60**
In search for the digital branding KPI...**62**
  Operationalization of the branding effect rather than direct sales
  evidence...62
  Digression: Advertising and advertising effectiveness 63
Quality contents are the key to branding budgets......................**64**
  High user engagement prevents pull-advertising reception 66
  External Networks and professional produced contents:
  Extending the combat zone 68
User data: The fight for the Cookie..**69**

**CHAPTER SIX: TECHNOLOGY HYPE CYCLE AND
THE LOGIN EFFECT**... **71**
Data-driven advertising and the technology hype cycle..............**72**
What goes up can't go down **73**
  Prisoners of their own customers: Branding further budgets in
  print and TV 74
  Organizational structure stifles innovation 74

CHAPTER SEVEN: HOW TO OVERCOME DISRUPTIVE CHALLENGES IN THE MEDIA MARKET ...76

Spin-off of independent units ...77
Conscious cannibalization of its core business ...77
Investment in the quality of digital content ...78
Arouse desires among users and advertisers ...78
The danger of a free event ...79
Digression: The digital crisis of the New York Times ...79
Adaptation of the disruptive technologies ...80
Translation of the branding-compatible ad formats to the digital offerings ...81
Performance-based billing based on KPI ...82
Click and view time as a uniform branding KPI ...83
Real-time bidding as digital-advertising operating system ...84
Recovery of the data equilibrium ...84
The ad ecosystem of the future ...85

CHAPTER EIGHT: A LOOK INTO THE CRYSTAL BALL ...87

Mobile: The next platform business ...88
Wandering path "second screen" ...90
TV: The replacement of the gatekeeper ...91
Facebook as program director ...91

BIBLIOGRAPHY ...93

Used and further reading ...93
Dossiers & White Papers ...93
Editorials ...94
Press Articles ...95

ABOUT THE AUTHOR ...98

Chapter One: Digital tsunami or mean high water?

Executive Summary

The ongoing digitization and the introduction of the Internet are the main drivers of innovation of our time. However, traditional media companies such as newspaper and magazine publishers and private TV channels have great difficulty adapting their business models to the new realities. While new competitors such as Google, Facebook, Apple, and Amazon dominate the digital business on the Internet, the established media companies can hardly monetize their digital content. This development shows clear parallels to a phenomenon that Harvard Professor Clayton Christensen described in his theory of disruptive innovations already in 1997.

Christensen's model can help to identify a pattern behind the seemingly chaotic upheavals in today's media landscape and at the same time show the blind spot of the operating companies.

Tsunamis are extremely treacherous natural phenomenon. Triggered by tectonic plate shifts under water, huge energies are passed in long waves from water molecule to water molecule over thousands of kilometers and are hardly distinguished via the naked eye from normal water movement. Only when the tsunami waves hit the coastal regions of the affected ocean, the extent of their destructive power becomes visible.

In his book *The Innovators Dilemma*, Harvard Professor Clayton M. Christensen analyzed the consequences of such technological tsunami waves in the form of disruptive innovations.[1] Why do great companies fail in the competition for innovation, even though they do everything right, they watch their competition, and ask their customers or have impressive R&D budgets? Nevertheless, they lose their market leadership when groundbreaking changes in technologies or market structures occur.

Christensen presented the results of his research in 1997, at a time when the Internet was still in its infancy. He illustrates those results with the development of steam and sailing ships in the early nineteenth century. His research results apply toward the structural changes triggered by the digitization and the triumph of the Internet. Just like the steam engine, which was a growing base of other innovations due to the new mobile availability of energy, the onset of digitization since the early 1990s has caused a paradigm shift in the industry's history.

Digitization as driver of innovation

The almost complete digitization of the world's stored information set took place in less than ten years during the turn of the millennium. In 1993, only 3 percent of all information was stored digitally; in 2007, it was already 94 percent. This puts the Digital Revolution on par with the Industrial Revolution of 200 years ago.[2] With it, the transition from the almost unlimited availability of energy to the almost unlimited availability of information is often referred to as the "fifth Kondratieff cycle," respectively.[3]

---

[1] Christensen, Clayton M. (1997): *The innovator's dilemma: when new technologies cause great firms to fail*, Boston, Massachusetts, USA

[2] Thierse, Wolfgang (2003): Lecture preserving tradition and modernization - social democracy in the decision, Leipzig, Germany

[3] Kondratieff, Nikolai D. (1926): *The long waves in the economy*, in: Archives for Social Science and Social Policy, Heidelberg, Germany, P. 56 et seqq.

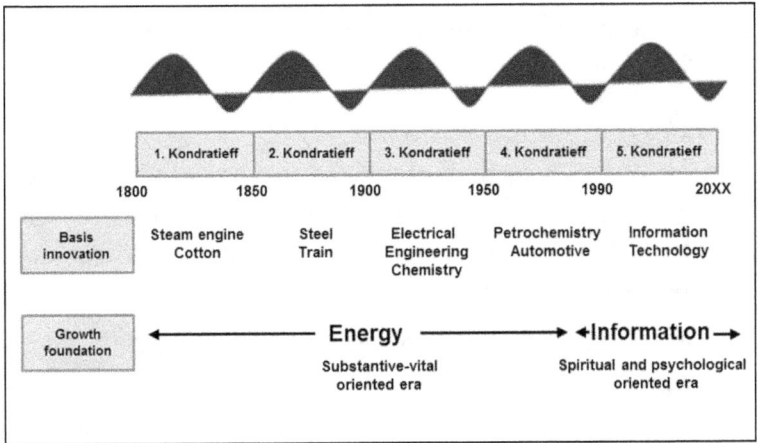

Figure 1: Kondratieff cycles over time.
Source: Weiber, Rolf (2008): The Empirical Laws of the Network Economy: The Effects of IT innovations on the economic framework, gleaning for participants in the high school forum PHW, Zurich p. 4.

There is no shortage of examples of the displacement of established companies in the context of digitization. With the emergence of digital photography, a whole industry nearly faltered and led to the bankruptcy of industry leader Kodak. People are not taking fewer pictures than before, rather the contrary. Nevertheless, Kodak and other film and camera manufacturers failed to respond to the challenges of the new digital technologies. The decline of Brockhaus is another example of digital disruption. Wikipedia has destroyed within a few years what the publisher had built in 200 years: the quasi-monopoly of encyclopedic knowledge. The introduction of iTunes and its consequences for the music market, online booking systems, and their impact on the travel agency industry, e-commerce vs. mail order — the list is endless. It has always created the same pattern: by the emergence of disruptive technologies, leading companies are relentlessly squeezed out of the market by new competitors.

In relation to the digitization, the Internet works as a catalyst to speed up the transition tempo and has a particularly strong influence on the media industry with its fully digitalizable and distributable contents.

Attack from the net

With the ability to download movies directly for the home TV screen, Apple is creating a new market segment, which additionally promises considerable competition to traditional TV channels.

Apple dominates the market for digital paid content

With the set-top box Apple TV, Apple offers the opportunity to use iTunes content on television. Equipped with the typical Apple features such as high-quality design and easy user guidance, the remote control of the Apple TV device consists of a small, elegant aluminum casing with just four buttons. Thus the user can navigate through the user interface optimized for simple operation, which is perfectly matched to the remote control. Here the formula "Apple users' high household income = high willingness to pay for quality content" seems to be coming true - at least, if the revenue that is earned by Apple with its iTunes offer is considered.

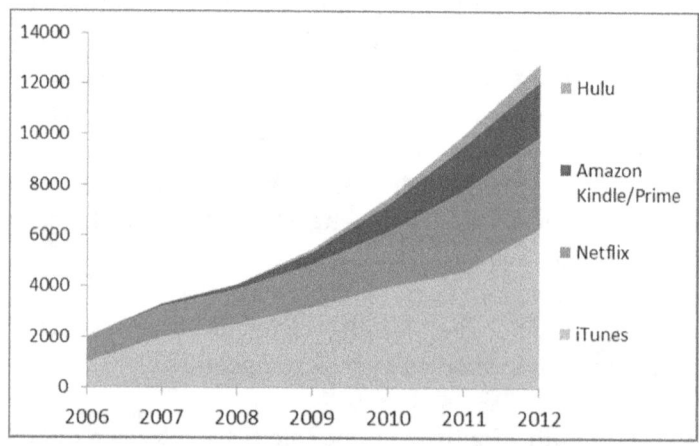

Figure 2: Revenues from digital content in the USA in 2011 in millions of US dollars.
(Source: Business Insider, Companies)

With the combination of devices, software, and media services, the company has established its own ecosystem for paid content and significantly dominates the field of paid content platforms in the United States.

Amazon morphs into a digital distribution platform

The same goes for Amazon, who discovered also how to sell digital content for itself, next to the e-commerce business with books, DVDs, and other media outlets. With the Amazon Kindle and the content service Amazon Prime, a subscription channel for video and Kindle content, Amazon expands into the digital distribution of content and creates its own ecosystem using the typical log-in effect for the user: Kindle content can only be accessed via Kindle devices.

Yet the established media houses with their premium content and established relations to Hollywood studios still hold a strong trump card. But to break through the phalanx between content distributors and TV stations, the new competitors increase their risk and start to create high-quality video content on their own expense. Kevin Spacey produced the award-winning TV series *House of Cards* exclusively for Netflix[4]. Amazon announced in the summer of 2013 to bring two comedy series and three children's programs at the start. The selection of the series was made on the basis of user feedback, after Amazon had aired several pilot programs in spring 2013. Amazon wants to bring out more productions in the future in this way. "The success of the first pilot tests have given us the impetus, to try the same approach with yet another series," citing Cnet Roy Price, head of Amazon Studios.[5] The first self-produced series, a political comedy

---

[4] Matyszczyk, Chris (2013): Netflix enjoys fine Kevin Spacey ad at White House dinner, published in CNET on the 28.08.2013, URL: http://news.cnet.com/8301-17852_3-57581791-71/netflix-enjoys-fine-kevin-spacey-ad-at-white-house-dinner/ Date: 10.07.2013

[5] Farber, Dan (2013): Amazon Studios debuts 14 pilots for free viewing, published online at 19.05.2013, URL: http://news.cnet.com/8301-1023_3-

with John Goodman, was a geek drama with four young app developers. Previously, Amazon also secured the rights of Stephen King's *Under the Dome* specifically for simultaneous publication as on TV. [6]

The shift of the branding budgets

In addition to the procurement market for content is that competition from the Internet is also growing on the advertising market. So far the Internet offers advertisers the ability to significantly boost its direct and e-commerce sales through search advertising and banner ads. In the first half of 2012, Google has achieved higher advertising revenue than all print media in the United States together.[7]

Google dominates the online advertising market almost monopolistic. The worldwide market share is at about 44 percent,[8] in some countries such as Germany over 70 percent[9]. Total revenues in the 2012 fiscal year were over US$50 billion - this is achieved almost exclusively through advertising.

But the new medium online has still not been established as a channel for the high-priced image and branding ad budgets, of which the traditional media companies deny their sales. Thus the established media companies with new competitors

---

57580146-93/amazon-studios-debuts-14-pilots-for-free-viewing,   Date: 30.07.2013

[6] Kafka, Peter (2013): Amazon Will Get New CBS Stephen King Series While It's Still on the Air, published on 11.02.2013 in AllthingsD, URL: http://allthingsd.com/20130211/amazon-will-get-new-cbs-stephen-king-series-while-its-still-on-the-air/ Date: 10.07.2013

[7] NAA, Pew Research Center (2012): Revenues of American newspapers with print and online advertising from 2003 to 2011 (in millions of US dollars), survey by Newspaper Association of America (NAA), Published by Pew Research Center's Project for Excellence in Journalism, March 2012

[8] Zenith Optimedia (2013): Top Thirty Global Media Owners 2013, URL: http://www.zenithoptimedia.com/zenith/shop/facts/top-thirty-global-media-owners-201/, Date: 10.07.2013

[9] Source: ZAW, PwC, OVK, search corresponds to Google's revenue with a search market share of 95%)

such as Google & Co. have been able to coexist relatively peacefully, without having been threatened in their core business. But now Google tries to expand its advertising model further apart from the previously dominant direct-sell campaigns and thereby surges into the core markets of established media companies. Facebook's advertising model is also increasingly attacking the classic branding budgets and setting a rapid growth in the day.

Should the new competitors actually manage to lure the brand advertising from print and TV in the digital channels, there would be a warm rain of money over the industry. In 2010, 33 percent of direct sales campaigns went online. In contrast, just 6 percent of the branding budgets went into the online channels.

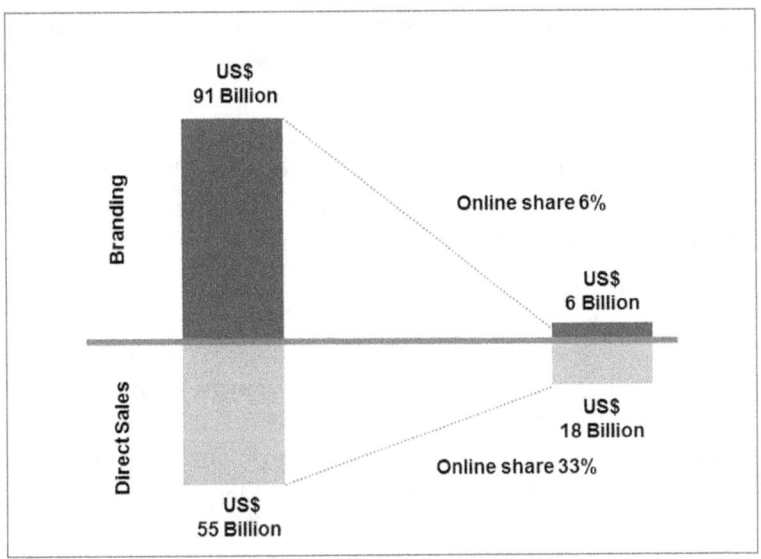

Figure 3: Distribution of branding and advertising sales in the United States by media channels.
(Source: Brand.net analysis, Barclays Capital, ThinkEquity Partners and DMA, Clipperton Finance, Numbers USA 2010)

The potential is enormous, and so Google's "Mr. Banner" Neil Mohan announced in 2011: "The market for online display advertising is about $ 30 billion worldwide. Let us together make a $ 200 billion market of it."[10] That such growth is only possible at the expense of traditional media budgets is clear.

Media managers are optimistic about the future

However, top managers of the media industry believe in a positive future. Although print editions have declined and the media consumption increasingly moves toward online, the mood seems to be optimistic. Maybe these managers are even secretly relieved. Despite all the gloomy end-time scenarios that experts and consultants to classic newspaper and magazine publishers had predicted for years, the corresponding consequences are far from failed. In fact, they are still doing relatively well from selling their content through the medium of print. But the publishers have mastered the dangers because: "The success of any new apps, and all new digital formats of distribution is dependent on the strong print brand," says Nicholas Coleridge, president of Condé Nast International.[11] "That's why we will never stop launching new magazines." Print will remain strong, according to the tenor of publishing managers.

Television managers have a similarly confident view on their industry: "I believe in the future of the media industry, and particularly in the future of television," says Gerhard Zeiler, president of Turner Broadcasting International and former head of the RTL Group, Europe's largest private TV group. He gave a confident keynote speech at the Media Days 2012 in

---

[10] Davis, Noah, (2011): Google VP Says Online Display Advertising Will Be A $200 Billion Market, published online at 15.09.2011 in Business Insider, Date: 02.09.2013, URL: http://articles.businessinsider.com/2011-09-15/tech/30158992_1_digital-channel-advertising-advertising

[11] Coleridge, Nicolas (2012): Presentation at the VDZ Publishers' Summit: Hubert Burda calls equal opportunity to compete, release date 08.11.2012, URL: http://www.printwirkt.de/pw-einzelansicht-5/hash/7d8eb474b202a64991af3575caab9c37/news/xuid Stand: 09.07.2013

Munich, Germany.[12] Using the example of Netflix, a US stock market listed company that provides movies by mail as well as offers video-on-demand digital streams, Zeiler explained that the established TV channels were not threatened by digitization and the web. Despite more than 20 million subscribers of Netflix in the United States, the number of traditional pay-TV households had not fallen.

Zeiler interpreted this as evidence for the thesis that new, innovative media businesses do not have to cause the death of traditional media. If they follow, they can even adapt to new business models. Indeed, there is no US cable company that does not offer new video-on-demand services in addition to its core business. It is considered a tsunami-safe strategy of traditional media provider competing with the digital challengers on their newly developed terrain.

For many of the participating media managers, it seems there is hope that the worst is already over and the danger was averted. The digital tsunami in their eyes is no longer a raging giant wave, but only a mean high water that can be defeated with a few sandbags. Very few believe that the previous waves are only precursors of a much more powerful giant wave that will strike a deep swath into the traditional media system and that requires much more radical actions to limit harm.

What Zeiler could not know at the time of his speech in the autumn of 2012: In December of the same year, Netflix announced that it secured the exclusive distribution rights from 2016 on of all future Walt Disney productions for a rumored US$300 million.[13] The deal includes all the content

---

[12] Zeiler, Gerhard (2012): "The new laws of the Media," International Keynote Munich Media Days, 24 October 2012, Munich, Germany

[13] Lawler, Rayen (2012): Netflix Strikes Streaming Deal With Disney, Gains Exclusive Access To New Titles Beginning In 2016, published online

from Disney, Walt Disney Animation Studios, Pixar Animation Studios, Marvel Studios, Disneynature, and all future Lucasfilm *Star Wars* episodes. Netflix had previously purchased content rights only long after the cinema, TV, and DVD distribution. With the new agreement, the Internet platform gets direct access to the content and can be used even before the TV broadcast. Thus Netflix significantly increases the value of its service to users and attacks the classic TV channels directly on their core business.

So far, market access restrictions such as transmitter licenses and high fixed costs were protecting the stations and their TV infrastructure, but this time is over and makes itself felt, especially in the TV rights purchase. The US station ESPN had to pay about US$700 million for the rights to broadcast Major League Baseball—that means almost twice as much money as the years before. [14]

Chaotic change or repetitive pattern?

Unlike traditional media companies, which are in a defensive movement from a drowning core business, the new competitors operate on the basis of functioning digital business models. The fatale for established media companies: the degree of approximation is no longer solely dependent on them, the Internet giant move to the high-margin premium markets of their offline competition. Meanwhile, the Davids have become the Goliaths. The new competitors are pushing increasingly aggressively in the core business of established media companies.

24.12.2012, URL: http://techcrunch.com/2012/12/04/netflix-disney/ date: 09.07.2013

[14] Frerker, Dr. Marcus (2013): everything everywhere—what consumers want and what media companies must adapt ", 5.6 billion U.S. dollars for MLB baseball rights till 2021 - TV / Radio, International, Mobile, McKinsey presentation on the Horizon Media Congress 2013, Frankfurt, Germany

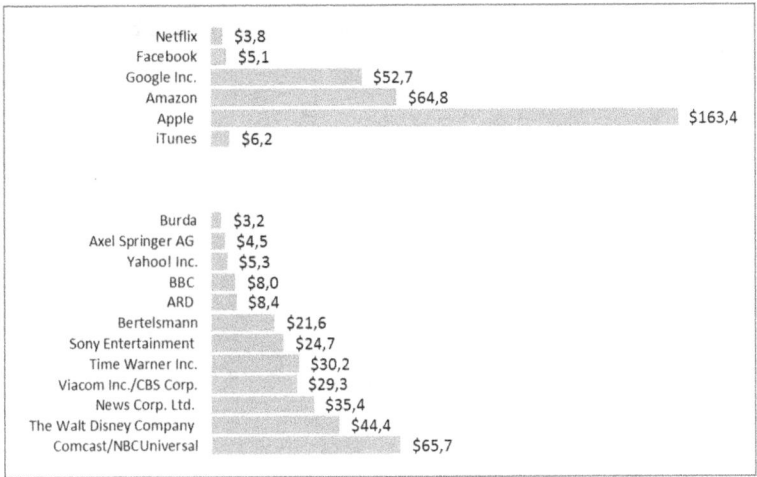

Figure 4: Revenues of selected media company in 2012 in billions US$
(Source: Company data, Institute for Media and Communications Policy)

Through the application of technology in the digital-distribution structures, the media industry changes from a local and national business into a globalized world in which everyone competes with everyone. In this conflict zone, private TV stations and magazine and newspaper publishers need to search for new digital business models.

The theory of disruptive innovations can help to get a clearer view of the laws of the seemingly chaotic upheaval here. The exciting thing about Christensen's theory is that it illuminates not only the winning side of such disruptive processes but deals mainly with the losers in this development. How could it happen that highly successful and innovative businesses fail, even though they have made the right from their subjective point of view of rational decisions to respond to the changes in the market? Simultaneously, Christensen offers recommendations for action on how the incumbents can overcome the disruptive challenges. This book tries to find the answers and show the blind spot of the actors and shows how the established media companies try to address the current challenges in typical but highly dangerous behavior that ultimately leads to failure.

Chapter Two: Christensen's model of disruptive innovations

Executive Summary

A disruptive innovation is an innovation that helps to create a new market and value network and goes on to disrupt an existing market and value network over a few years or decades, displacing an earlier technology.

Here the term "technology" refers not only to technical innovations; a change in the legal framework or a new business model can also represent disruptive innovations.

Only if established firms adapt the new technologies and cannibalize their own core business, they will have a chance to overcome the disruptive challenges.

To illustrate his theory, Christensen goes far back into the history of industrialization and reveals a pattern that always repeats itself when disruptive technologies occur. He uses the example of the rising steam navigation in the early nineteenth century, as the hitherto dominant sailing ships were superseded by the new steam ships. The amazing part: none of the manufacturers of sailing ships were apparently able to adapt to the new technologies early enough and also construct steam ships. Instead, the managers of the established sailing shipyards were more committed to the now outdated technology of the sail drive. Even as more and more steam ships were built, the sail yards invested heavily in the development of ever larger sailboats—unsuccessfully. Their ships could not compete with the superior drive technology of the new steamships. As on December 14, 1907, the largest ever-built sailing ship without an auxiliary drive came in a storm and capsized: "Not just a sailing ship had gone down, but an entire industry."[15]

In the ex-post analysis, the superiority of steam navigation seems understandable and logical. The interesting question is why the shipyard managers, who had been leading the sailing ships industry and built the biggest ships in the world, had not responded to the invention of the steam drive and miscalculated so incredible wrong in the assessment of this new technology? The new steam ships were directed to the same customers; they fulfilled the same functions, in principle, only much more efficient and cost effective.

Disruptive innovations create their own markets

The potential of disruptive technologies is difficult to detect in the early stages of development. New technologies initially often have serious shortcomings and cannot keep up after a first analysis of product characteristics. It is almost impossible to predict for established businesses which one of all the many new developments once will become a real threat to their core business. Often, these technologies also create their own markets or even develop their technological maturity in low-margin niche markets that are deliberately shunned by leading companies. The steamboats were preparing their future technological superiority on the low-margin market for inland waterways. For the much higher-margin ocean voyages, the new technology seemed technically completely unsuitable. In the beginning, steamboats were much slower than the sailing ships, needing in some cases a sail for an auxiliary drive, and its technology was prone to failure.

---

[15] Christensen, Clayton M. (1997): "The Innovator's Dilemma," P. 9

Prisoners of their own customers

Managers of the sail yards were therefore faced with the decision whether to invest in a technology that obviously had significant product defects and found only in a niche market where low margins used to be achieved. In addition, the shipping companies wanted to order no steamboats for shipping on the open sea because of technical deficiencies. Instead they ordered always bigger and faster sailing ships from the shipyards. The yard manager felt further confirmed to have acted properly. After Christensen, it is just this customer orientation that becomes one of the main sticking points in the proper handling of disruptive innovations. Most innovations are "evolutionary innovation," meaning developments that are based on the needs of customers. This type of innovation management is the daily bread of the company.

Upon the occurrence of disruptive innovations, such an approach, however, can be fatal. The customer focus is usually on the fact that the product meets certain requirements. He cannot judge whether an innovation will prevail. However, he will immediately replace all existing products and services, if they can provide a higher value or a lower price on a new technology. This makes it an extremely dangerous consultant for companies. Christensen says that companies make in this situation "a prisoner of the customer."[16]

What goes up can't go down

The login principle is another important point that further clarifies Figure 5. The disruptive technologies are at the lower end of the market, sometimes even in foreign market segments where product requirements are lower and turn lower margins. In order to earlier adapt such technology, the

---

[16] Christensen, Clayton M. (1997): "The Innovator's Dilemma," p. 45

incumbents would have to move almost in a downward motion toward the lower market segments. But this contradicts Christensen, basically, given the upward mobility of established companies.

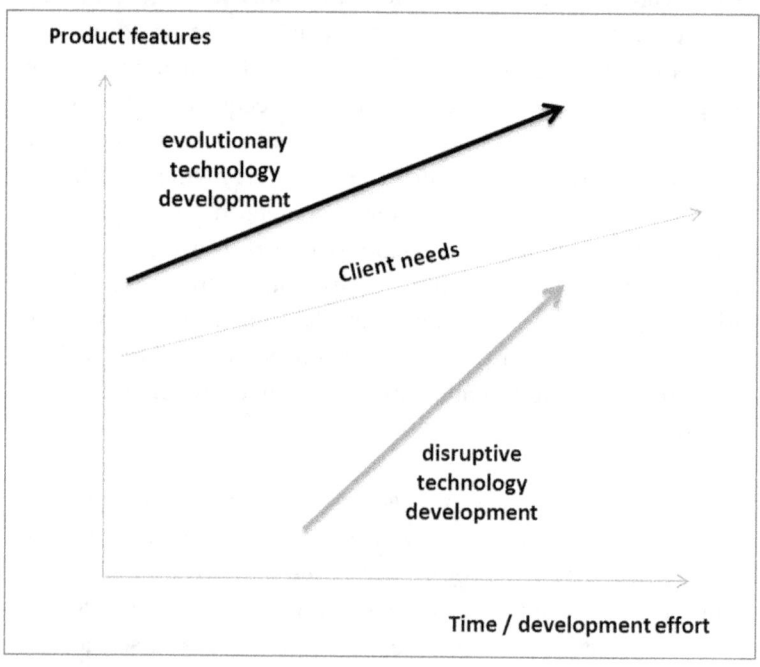

Figure 5: Development path of disruptive technologies.
(Source: based on Christensen, Clayton (1997): The Innovators Dilemma)

Because in order to satisfy their need for constant growth, which is especially required of shareholders, these companies need to grow in high-end markets with strong margins promised.

Therefore an expansion in upper-premium segments of the market seems more promising. It is a kind of *over-engineering* in which the product functionalities are further increased, albeit at significantly increasing development and production costs. At the same time, the customer benefits are *over met*. It creates a kind of vacuum that is easily filled by the disruptive technology. Suddenly, it is able to satisfy customer needs at much lower cost.

Also business models are technologies

Christensen's concept of technology includes everything that allows a business to meet a specific customer need. This can include special product features or innovative pricing models; they can range from specific forms of services to innovative marketing and sales techniques. Often, the individual components must not only reinvent the company; a customer-oriented combination of existing products and services is sufficient to create a disruptive technology.

Christensen's examples range from sailing ships to the dredging industry and low-cost airlines to manufacturers of computer drives. In all these examples, a new disruptive technology comes on the scene, which occurs after a phase of technological maturity in high-margin markets where it can meet the customer needs at a lower price. Although the established companies develop their products with all the force, they cannot compete with the much steeper innovation curve of development of the new technologies and lose market share or are completely pushed out of the market.

Chapter Three: The innovator's dilemma of the traditional media companies

Executive Summary

The traditional media companies so far cannot successfully monetize their online coverage. As described in Christensen's model, they have great difficulty adapting to the new technologies in the form of the return-channel-based ad delivery. Instead, they do not deliver their ads user-based, but rely on the traditional one-way audience targeting through content. This leads to poor and unsatisfactory advertising performance results in the form of low click-through rates.

Disappointed by the poor monetization potential of their digital content, many of the established media companies turn away and fall into a typical pattern also described by Christensen. They invest in evolutionary innovations and try to steer ad budgets in the old print and TV channels, thereby protecting their core business.

As a result, brand advertising budgets mostly remain in the established TV and print channels of the established media companies.

Especially newspaper and magazine publishers have had high hopes for the online businesses in the recent years. While ad spending on print advertising has declined steadily for years, online is the only segment of the advertising market that can show steady growth. That this market growth is fed primarily from Google's search advertising business, the established media companies are increasingly feeling bitter.

The main problem of established companies dealing with disruptive innovation is the lack of adaptation of new technologies and business models. This pattern is also evident when looking at the established media companies trying to handle the new possibilities of the return channel.

The return channel as disruptive basis innovation

Online advertising such as banner ads has existed since 1994. The first banner was online on October 27, 1994, on the site HotWired, the online forerunner of *Wired* magazine. The client was the US telecommunications giant AT&T.[17]

Figure 6: The first banner ad ever.
(Source: AdAge, Hotwired)

---

[17] D'Angelo, Frank (2009): Happy Birthday, Digital Advertising! – The Banner Campaign that Started a $24 billion Business, and Got a 78 Prozent Click-through Rate, published on 26.10 2009 online in Adage, URL: http://adage.com/digitalnext/post?article_id=139964, Date: 10.07.2013

HotWired thus coined the term "banner ad" and was the first advertising medium that provided its customers a performance record in the form of click-through rate of the advertisement.

Ken McCarthy, Internet pioneer of the first hour and an early promoter of the commercialization of the Internet through online advertising, saw at the time a paradigm shift in traditional purchasing advertising ahead. He was convinced there would be a break in the industry through the measurability of the banners and the possibility of clicks. "The direct-response model in which the return on investment (ROI) of each advertising medium can be measured is the only sustainable business model for advertising.2[18]

Inclusion of users reaction in real time

The return channel enables the bi-directional exchange of information between the transmitter and the receiver—this data on the reaction of the receiver to the advertising message can be evaluated in real time. From the perspective of advertisers, the Internet has a big advantage over traditional media.

Comparing the conventional media to online advertising, it behaves similarly to fishing. Traditional advertising media without a return channel fish with large trawl. They throw out their nets, and only if the net is brought back on board, fishermen can see if the desired species of fish was caught. The by-catch is thrown back overboard—as long as enough quality fish are in the net, it is well worth the drive. Although the fishermen try to optimize the catch through the selection of the fishing grounds and the right size of net meshes, the cost of fuel and crew remain the same, even if the net is empty. In print and TV media that does not have a direct feedback

---

[18] Comm, Joel (2008). Click Here to Order: The World's Most Successful Internet Marketing Entrepreneurs, Morgan James, San Francisco

channel, the results of an advertising placement can always be identified as in the example of the fishing only in retrospect and by sample projections.

Advertising with a return channel is more like fishing with bait and hooks. The fisherman tries different lures. When the fish bites, the fisherman knows he has found the right bait. In such a way he can mass deploy the right bait on the hook. But the bite of the fish, so the click, is still no absolute guarantee of success because the fish can still go off the hook. It is only an indication that the fisherman has found the right bait. The right landing of the fish remains abandoned to its fate.

Sharing the investment risk
The choice of billing method for advertising at the same time also determines the distribution of the investment risk between advertiser and publisher.

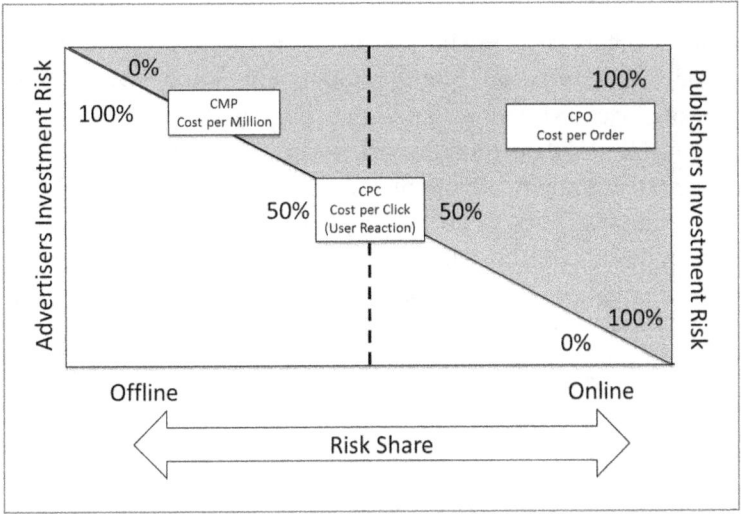

Figure 7: Distribution of investment risk between advertisers and publisher.
(Source: author illustration)

Media channels, which have no direct return channel, are billed through the so-called cost per million (CPM) pricing model. The customer is paying for advertising displayed to a certain number of people. Since there is no direct measurability of the user reaction to his ad, he must rely on his review samples and projections. The investment risk thus remains with the advertisers.

The new digital advertising media with return channel is different. The reaction of the recipient to the advertising message is immediate and directly measurable. Thus accounting models are possible that work related to the advertising performance. What such a model means therefore—in contrast to traditional print media and TV—is a real risk split between advertisers and advertising.

The transfer of the established models

But the established media companies soon turned away from a performance-based billing model, apparently with good reason. The first banner on a news page had a click-through-rate (CTR) of 78 percent. But the fascination of the user for the hitherto unknown advertising faded quickly; however, the click rates fell rapidly in the sequence. Meanwhile, the click-through rate (CTR) is 0.01 percent for a standard banner. That means only one of 100,000 delivery banners reaches a user and makes it so curious that he would like to learn more about the offer.

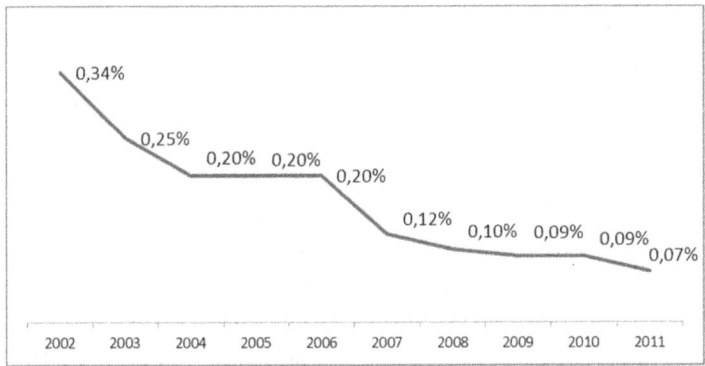

Figure 8: Development of the CTR of standard banners.
(Source: Clipperton Finance Analysis, MediaMind, eMarketer, Pearson)

The move away from the click

The move away from the click and the related performance-based billing is probably the most far-reaching wrong decision in the history of online advertising. Because of this decision, the established media companies never adopted the return-channel-driven advertising model. Until today, all major digital marketers of publishers and TV channels sell their media through CPM models they learned from the offline business: they speak about the so-called "premium" model. But with this fixed-price model, they ignore the return channel, the lack of user feedback on their banners and leave the investment risk completely with their advertisers.

So here a vicious cycle emerges: instead of improving click-through rates and developing effective performance-based formats, they settle up the upfront payment model. Like this, the publishers have no reason to optimize the performance measurements of the banner. They rolled their own problem simply over to their advertising clients. But since the performance evidence in the form of low click-through rates are so bad, and there are no other established evaluation criteria, it is difficult for the media agencies to invest in the new advertising channels. Nevertheless, the digital marketing stiffens their premium approach: they keep prices artificially high and hope that the Gordian knot will burst some day, and the warm rain of brand advertising money may finally pour out on them.

By this refusal of a performance-based billing model for branding campaigns by the publishers, a large part of their digital ad inventory stays empty and for sale. It is an absurd situation: the home pages for a few large sites are sold out for weeks, as they are set as an offshoot of the strong print brands in the media planner's minds. Industry insiders speak of so-called "executive bookings," which shows more concern that the respective head of marketing or advertising customer looks to the start of the campaign on the homepage of the websites of that strong print brands—and less to the computationally verifiable return of digital media performance.

The emergence of ad networks and arbitrage

To monetize their empty display inventories, the digital marketers started to work with ad networks. Ad networks are nothing more than middlemen who make their profits through arbitrage effects. They buy large contingents from the publishers at dumping prices and pay in advance by CPM prices, often with discounts up to 80 percent and more. The ad networks then sell the inventory for advertisers to turn on, but this time on the basis of performance-based models such as cost-per-click. If they are able to optimize the click-through rates by user data and targeting, they create an arbitrage profit, which they do not need to pass on to the media companies due to the fixed-price agreement. For the individual publishers and website operators, this model does not change their fundamental problem: they stick to their high sunk costs for the content creation while the ad networks enrich themselves on the media companies inventory.

The reach paradigm

Paradoxically, despite all the problems, a veritable race about the most far-reaching title on the Internet has started in the past. For years, online was the medium with the greatest promise of growth, and each manager who claimed otherwise had a difficult time. So managers were constantly working on expanding the reach through their digital publications. The result is an oversupply of available display ads that pushes the prices even further down. Instead of producing quality content, publishers tried to achieve a high number of page views with a minimum of investments. In contrast to the print counterparts, the online editors rarely have the opportunity to make a journalistic product of such high quality that readers are willing to pay money for it. It was indeed never asked of them: range has been the decisive factor.

Chapter Four: Data-driven advertising as a disruptive innovation

Executive Summary

How a disruptive technology can successfully develop on the basis of the return channel is shown by Google. The inclusion of the bi-directional exchange of information on the reaction of the recipient of the advertising message played a crucial role in the success of the Google model. Like this the company has created its own market segment. The introduction of data-driven ad serving through Google's search ads is also the birth of data-driven advertising.

With the quality of data from Facebook and the development of real-time bidding as an open-data exchange standard, data-driven advertising has now reached the next stage in the technological development path of this disruptive innovation.

Larry Page and Sergey Brin, the two founders of Google, first met at Stanford University and pursued a more scientific approach in developing their search engine. They focused on the quality of search results, giving the user experience the highest priority. Though the Google home page today lists more than 100 million unique visitors every day and represents a media value of tens of millions of dollars, it is still completely ad-free. Only on the results page of the search you will find the small text ads, which helped Google to generate a turnover of US$50 billion and a profit of over US$10 billion in 2012.[19]

Google strictly separates the organic results of its search algorithms from advertisements. Google's managers were

---

[19] Google Business Report 2012

always aware that an independent search result, free from manipulation, is the foundation of its business model. Once the results were manipulated by some advertisers, the search would lose its credibility and no longer be used. This self-understanding results in the most famous Google motto: "Don't be evil."

The Google model

From a formal point of view, Google acts as a traditional media company as a mediator between advertiser and audience. Google only doesn't produce any journalistic articles or television series to generate the content to catch user attention, employs no journalists, editors, and TV producers — all is done instead by the search algorithm.

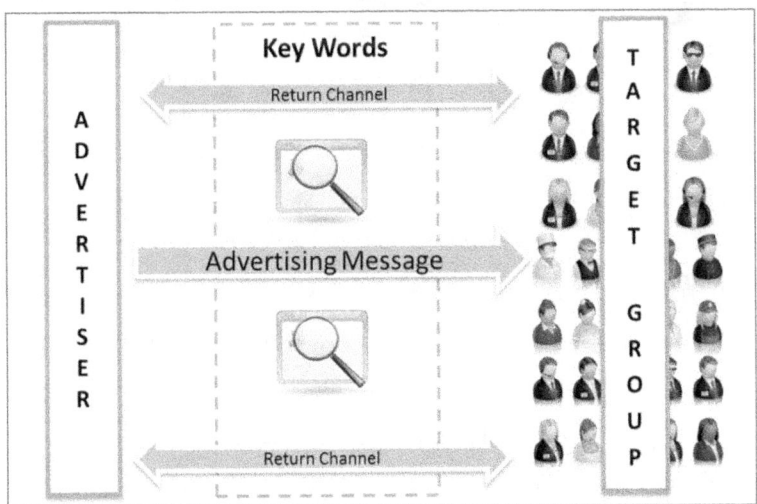

*Figure 9: Google as an advertising medium and intermediary
of attention.*
(Source: author illustration)

The search results automatically generated by the Google system for each search query by the user ultimately meet the same task as the content expensively produced by the established media companies: they captivate the attention of the user and can be combined with the advertising messages of advertisers.

The grandsons of Adam Smith

Google's pricing model is a real-time auction mechanism, the purest form to create market equilibrium between demand and supply. Like this, Google's advertising model seems to have sprung from the textbook of neoclassical economics.

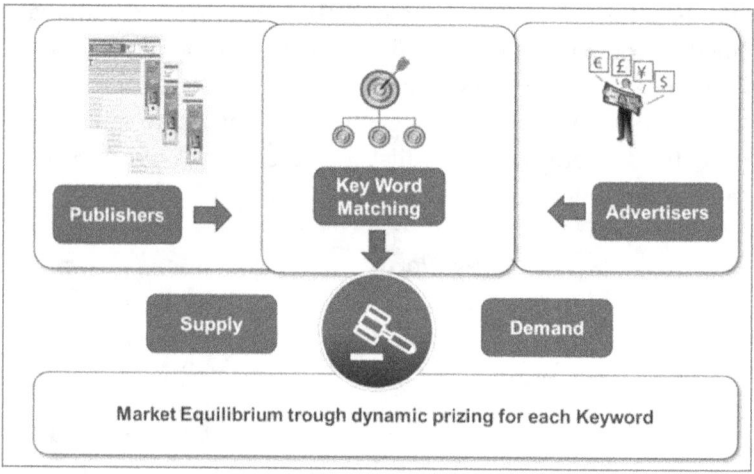

Figure 10: The Google display model.
(Source: author illustration)

Supply and demand meet in a perfectly groomed market to determine the price for each display ad in a dynamic auction process. Google uses the Vickrey auction where the advertiser only pays a cent more than the so-called next lowest bid. Former Google competitors such as the search provider Overture had tried a different model, such as the "second highest bid," which favors the seller. But that meant that buyers were constantly trying to lower their bids and the ad revenue decreases.

The search as a pre-filter for interested buyers

From the advertiser's point of view, an extremely effective pre-filtering takes place solely through the use of a search engine. Ads that are displayed in the search engine of Google do reach users who actually are interested in buying a product or a service. Internet users only use about 4 percent of their time with the actual search on the net. The rest of the time they write emails, read articles, watch videos, shop online, or surf social networks.[20] Again only a small part of these searches is even interesting for the Google advertising model, but still enough to refinance the billions of advertising dollars.

From a financial perspective, search queries motivated by an intention to buy are of interest to Google. Almost every online purchase starts today with the entry of a product name or service in the search box of Google. People type a product name, a manufacturer, or a product type into a Google search in order to further inform, compare prices, to fight through postings, or to find reviews. Ads that appear in this context are highly relevant and sometimes even perceived as useful as the organic search results of the search algorithm. If a query has a commercial intent and thus puts a purchase intention behind the use of the search engine, over 64 percent of the clicks go to advertisements and not to the actual search results. At the same time, users take advertising as even more true as enrichment rather than as a disturbing element. Correspondingly, these ads have high CTR and success rates.

Data to increase advertising relevance

The databased delivery of their display ads is a critical component of Google's success. Instead of offering a driftnet, Google offers an automated, highly scalable, and self-optimizing mega fishing route. Once a user enters a query into the search slot, Google automatically displays the search results and the matching and relevant "advertising baits." The click corresponds to the bite of the fish and is the basis of the performance-based billing model.

---

[20] comScore (2012) comScore Media Matrix, Worldwide 2007-2011

And only through the use of data from the reaction of the users to the ads, can Google target accuracy and ensure the ad quality so that the advertisement also applies to the right audience. Even if the user does not click on the ad, the Google algorithm tracks this behavior and offers another advertising display ad the next time the same query search is executed.

Google also differentiates between "long clicks" and "short clicks." If a user clicks on an ad and then does not return directly back to the search page, Google will assume that the ad was helpful: it slides up the ranking. If the user returns immediately after clicking an ad again on the search page and clicks on another ad or an organic link, the ad will be scaled down in order of relevance. Even if an advertiser is willing to pay more money per ad, the better clicked, the more useful user ad is preferred.

Google educates its advertisers

At the beginning of its advertising program, Google followed the established roles of the advertising industry. Google hired Tim Armstrong, an experienced ad salesman, and opened an office in New York, the center of the American advertising industry. Ads were sold on the CPM-mode. The advertiser paid for his advertising—if a user clicked or didn't click on the advertisements was irrelevant. Then the system was changed, and the advertisers should now pay per click. Google's managers had realized they could achieve extremely high click-through rates by combining the ads with the search results. Instead of accepting the established advertising models, Google executives identified two important relationships: the importance of clicks as a measurement for advertising success and the importance of proper integration of the advertising format in the user experience.

Advertisers that faced the new system from Google, with its small text ads already critical, first ran against this change and canceled their bookings. But soon they became aware of the advantage of the new system. Google prevailed with its innovation, ultimately also for the benefit of advertisers. A crucial factor for the success of the program was the steady improvement of the ad quality. Google is forcing its advertisers to choose their ad text and key words so that they achieve a certain minimum CTR. If this click-through rate is not reached, the display is switched off—a real revolution. Advertisers were used that their ads were always delivered, as long as they paid for and were not contrary to the advertising standards. That the user suddenly had an indirect influence was initially met with total ignorance from many advertising managers. But in the end, Google sat through anyway and the success showed that the company was right.

Google advertising and the AIDA model

Looking at the Google offer within the classic AIDA model, the difference from the traditional TV and print advertising becomes particularly clear.

Digression: The AIDA model

Companies use advertising to sell their products. They are therefore willing to take long detours in the communication if the end leads to boost of sales of their own products. Probably the most widely used model for the way of advertising is called the AIDA model. Lecturer, author, and teacher Elmo Lewis has described this still up-to-date theory in an article on advertising in 1898 for the first time. It stands for the English terms attention, interest, desire, and action (activity).

Attention
The customer's attention is excited.
Interests
The customer's interest is aroused. He is interested in the product.
Desire
The desire for the product is awakened. Owning request is triggered.
Action
The customer buys the product (at best).

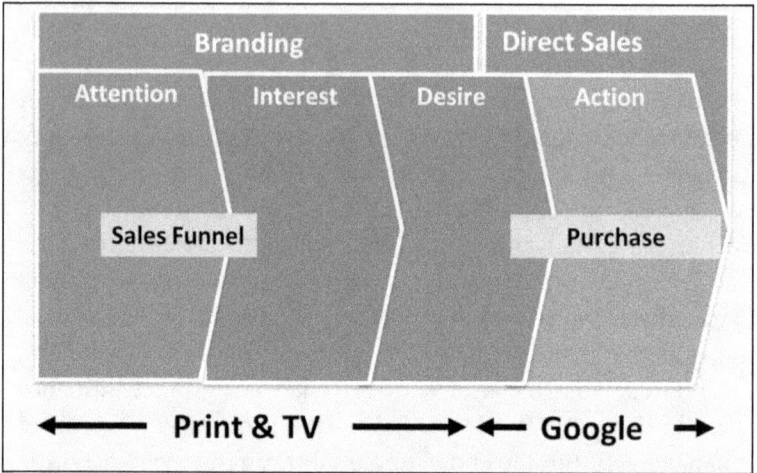

Figure 11: Google Ads within the AIDA model
(Source: author illustration)

The first three of the above goals can be summarized under branding or brand building. A company makes its name or a product known and associates it with positive emotions. If the name is established, a positive image of the brand should influence the possible purchase decision, and ideally the recipient of the advertising messages opts for the advertised product.

Branding: Attention strength, increase brand awareness, emotional and positive charging of the brand.

Direct Sales: Initiating a direct purchase action.

During the early stages of the AIDA model (attention, interest, desire, and action), which is primarily used print and TV advertising, search engine advertising is particularly well suited to potential customers who have already made a purchase decision and are on the search for a specific product.

Ad spending per usage time unit

With the combination of data usage to increase relevancy of the advertising and the performance-based billing, including the return channel, Google managed to create an extremely efficient form of advertising.

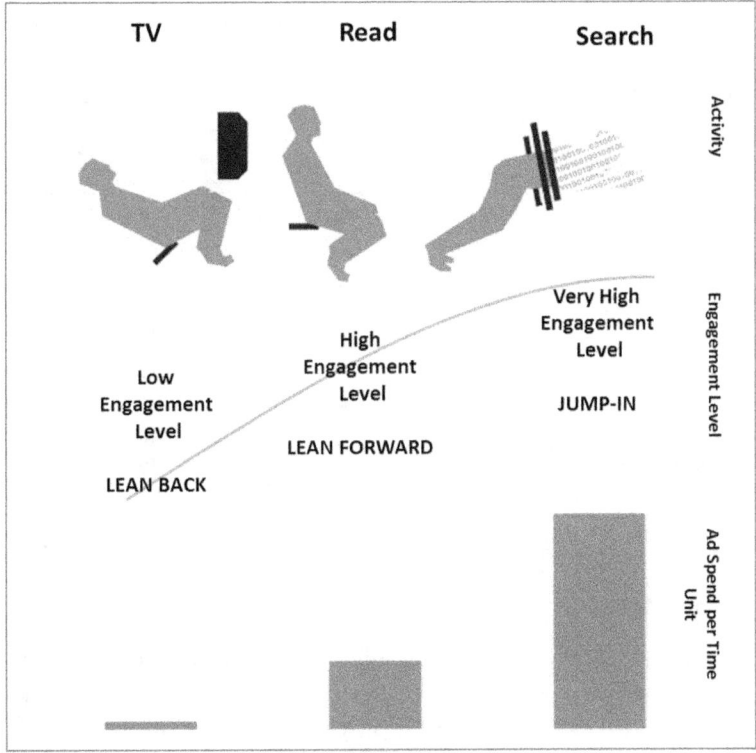

Figure 12: Advertising spending per minute media use.
(Source: ARD / ZDF, ZAW, OVK, PwC, ComScore; author illustration inspired by TrendOne)

Here the correlation between user engagement and advertising models is also clear. Thus the study of the medium of television is relatively passive. In view of the fact that people today are on average about 220 minutes per day watching television, the advertising expenditure per minute media consumption is relatively low. In magazines and newspaper reading, the engagement level is much higher. The leader is search advertising, with a very high engagement level and most ad spending per time unit.

Search engine marketing as a direct sales tool

Google has established itself as an advertising medium,
especially for direct sales advertising. It offers advertisers the
opportunity to boost their e-commerce sales directly and
measurably in real-time.

Advertiser	Branch	Google Ad Revnenues 2011 in Million US$
Lowes	eCommerce	59,1
Amazon	eCommerce	55,2
The Home Depot	eCommerce	50,3
University of Phoenix	E-Learning	46,9
Statefarm	Insurance	43,7
Progressive	Insurance	43,1
eBay	eCommerce	42,8
AT&T	Telco	40,8
Booking.com	Travel	40,4
Macy´s	eCommerce	35,6

Figure 13: The biggest Google advertisers in the United States
in 2011.
(Source: WordStream 2011)

A glance at the list of the biggest advertisers of Google
illustrates this. On the top ten, you will find only providers of
goods and services that can be purchased on the Internet.

The technological s-curve

Google with its return channel-driven display model for direct sales ads created a separate market, which is, according to Christensen, another typical characteristic of a disruptive technology. The sales-oriented advertising market provided an ideal environment for the data-driven advertising to develop and advance their technology maturity. The return channel provides advertisers immediate success monitoring in real-time supplied in the form of clicks, a simple but effective proof of performance for the advertising effect. The new technology of data-driven advertising has evolved outside the Google platform.

Real-time bidding: The Google model into a thousand pieces

Real-time bidding (RTB) makes the key features of data data-driven advertising available outside of the Google platform. Real-time bidding works as a communications protocol or transmission standard. Various individual companies take over the respective subtasks of the original Google system to deliver data-driven advertising and auction by auction. RTB allows communicating and exchanging information about users, advertising formats and prices within milliseconds. The auction of the display is a multistep process that goes through the following steps[21]:

1. A user visits a website. Is the advertising inventory on this website connected via a sell-side platform or the ad server to the real-time bidding system, the user and the advertising placement can be offered to interested advertisers.

---

[21] Schroeter, Dr. Andreas, (2012): The Future of Display Advertising, Hamburg, Germany

2. *The advertisers can use so-called demand-side platforms (DSP) to bid on the user. To determine the value of the user and the advertising placement, the DSP detects cookies stored on the user's computer and matches them with the publisher's own databases (data management platforms/DMP).*

3. *The sell-side platforms (SSPs) take on the supply side bids and give the impression to the highest bidder. The advertising of the highest bidder will appear in the advertising slot.*

There are two main technical challenges: first, the parties need to take a large number of requests and answers. Second, the whole process, despite this number of requests, must be very fast, since the user should not be annoyed by a slow-loading website. The entire bidding process usually takes no longer than 100 milliseconds.[22]

Strategic positioning within the real-time advertising market

In the market for data-driven advertising, there are several strategies on how to position the individual vendor. It also comes down to who is going to pay them at the end for their service. The most attractive position for a technology provider is the marketplace or ad exchanges. Because here they can get not only paid for their technology services but also for the *matchmaking*, bringing together supply and demand. Also the matchmaker can determinate his own remuneration, as he creates a certain black box where nobody other than himself knows the real matching price.

---

[22] Schroeter, Dr. Andreas (2012): The future of Display Advertising, Hamburg, Germany

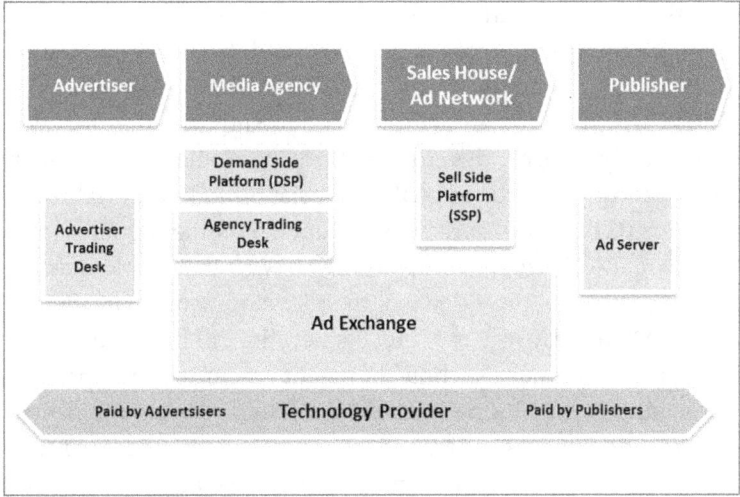

Figure 14: Value chain and market participants in real-time advertising market.
(Source: author illustration)

The ad exchange model

Right Media, a start-up founded in 2003 in New York, was the first advertising platform that has been tried on an automated advertising marketplace model outside of Google. At a time when the hope still rested on an early shift of branding budgets toward online, and Google was also busy trying to build its own AdWords system, the Right Media offer was promising. Even so promising that Yahoo announced on April 30, 2007, to take over the company for US$850.[23] But Yahoo's bet was not on today. Since Yahoo itself has never developed a proprietary technology that could even come close to the quality of the data of Google's search, Yahoo was missing an important building block for success. The idea of the ad marketplace never really took off.

---

[23] Arrington, Michael (2007): Panama Not Enough To Battle Google: Yahoo Acquires RightMedia, published in TechChrunch 29. April 2007, URL: http://techcrunch.com/2007/04/29/panama-not-enough-to-battle-google-yahoo-acquires-rightmedia/, Date 01.07.2013

For the future of automated ad trading, three names would play an important role, which emerged from Right Media: Mike Nolet, Brian O'Kelley, and Boris Mouzykantskii (Dr. Boris). All three were employed at Right Media for the technical platform development. Mike Nolet as product manager and director of analytics, Brian O'Kelley as technical director (CTO), and Boris Mouzykantskii as the owner of the software development company IPONWEB that worked as an external service provider on the development platform of Right Media. How close the cooperation of the three was shows a common technical patent awarded to predict probabilities for individual bids in the real-time bidding process, which was registered under patent number 7908238 on August 31, 2007, for the names Michiel Nolet, Charles Brian O'Kelley, and Boris Mouzykantskii.[24]

However, the three parted ways after the sale of Right Media again. Brian O'Kelley and Mike Nolet left Right Media shortly after the acquisition, and also working with IPONWEB was soon terminated by Yahoo. While O'Kelley and Nolet founded AppNexus to build their own ad exchange and thus officially step into the ring with Google, Yahoo & Co., "Dr. Boris" further concentrated to license its technology platform to other companies. IPIONWEB grows in the shade of the ad tech boom from its own revenues without venture capital or IPO plans. Although already several technology start-up companies whose technology is based on their technology platform were sold for tens of millions US dollars, IPONWEB still acts itself in the background.

AppNexus, however, is now fully in the spotlight of the current development. With Michael Rubenstein, former VP and general manager at Google's DoubleClick, a top manager could be lured away from Google. In the background,

---

[24] US Patent registry (2007): Patent number US 11/848,688 URL: http://www.google.de/patents/US7908238?hl=de, Date 10.07.2013

Microsoft is also heavily involved. Through his involvement in AppNexus, they finally tried to play a significant role in the world of online advertising. With a D financing round in February 2013, the company raised a total amount of US$140 million from venture capital; an IPO is planned for no later than 2014. [25]

AppNexus pursued the development of its market place from the beginning with a special strategy, which made it difficult for many of the competitors to recognize the early competition, while creating clear dependencies. So the company turned first to media agencies and advertisers to establish its own platform as a media-planning tool for display ad campaigns. When they had enough demand in the form of agencies and advertisers collected, AppNexus extended its range and also offered publishers and website operators to automate their ad inventory sales on the AppNexus platform. Thus the New York technology company itself created a competitive advantage over other technology providers, which now had to be connected to AppNexus as a demand partner to access the advertising budgets of the agencies that were using the AppNexus platform. But AppNexus is not the only horse in the race. More heavily funded start-up companies, such as PubMatic and Rubicon Project, are fighting with Google and Yahoo for supremacy in the automated online advertising market.

Supply-side and demand-side platforms

Other technology providers focus on just one page within the online advertising market. Supply-side platforms (SSPs) are working for media companies and publishers who enable their advertising inventory through these technologies for the real-time advertising market. And here also the big boys of the

---

[25] Adexchanger (2011): CEO Mouzykantskii Says IPONWEB Expanding Media Trading Tech Business Globally, published in Adexchanger on 05.12.2011, URL: http://www.adexchanger.com/online-advertising/iponweb/, Date10.07.2013

industry have their fingers in the pie. Improve Digital, which was founded by the Dutch entrepreneurs Janneke Niessen and Joelle Frijters in 2008 in Amsterdam, has belonged to the Swiss Publigroupe since end of 2012. The German company Yieldlab was founded by United Internet, one of the biggest Internet-holding companies in Europe. These new competitors compete with the established marketplace operators and the classical Adserver providers who are also connecting their system to real-time bidding connections.

However, the actual upgrade takes place on the part of media agencies. In addition to technology-independent providers of demand-side platforms (DSP), the media agencies invest heavily in technology. They set up their own subsidiaries such as Xaxis (GroupM) or Annalect (Omnicom), the agency trading desks to make use of user data to qualify campaigns and target them precisely. And also big advertisers are just beginning to develop their own trading desks to take advantage of data-driven advertising.

From key word to user targeting

Ultimately the concept gained momentum in the market with an innovation that originated in France. A company called Criteo, founded in Paris in 2005, established a working database and a viable alternative to Google's search data. Thus it is possible to derive a user's purchasing intentions without having to rely on the search engine Google data. Re-targeting is a simple but effective principle. If a user visits an online website, product offers appears on third-party websites as a display advertising banner after the visit. The website owner prolongs his sales counter, and offers will be sent to the customer after he leaves the shop. Despite a lot of negative criticism and complaints of shoes that seem to be following users through the Internet after visiting a Zappos or Zalando online shop, the success of the principle is undoubted.

Re-targeting data refers to a direct action of a user and is therefore highly up-to-date. There is a measurable effect on the click-through rate of banners and the subsequent sell-through rates, in contrast to almost all other approaches. It does not matter if someone is male or female, big or small, old or young: who has visited the online store or the website of a particular company has a relatively high probability to be also interested in its products. The average click rate of Criteo banners is 0.7 percent. A remarkable value, it is compared with the average of a standard banner ad click-through rate without databased delivery of currently average 0.01 percent.[26]

Facebook: Exhibitionism as part of the system

With Facebook, another player has entered the field, which heralds the next evolution of data-driven advertising with its unprecedented wealth of data. Facebook users decorate their virtual profiles with all sorts of information: it indicates which music groups someone likes, preferred vacation destinations, which movie someone has particularly enjoyed, or which is his or her favorite bar. All this information is used to bring your own personality expressed on the profile or show a belonging to a particular social group. At the same time, these data provide the marketers with an incredibly rich playing field to observe their target audiences and accurately adjust their advertising campaigns. Also social relationships can be clustered and mapped to probabilities in preferences and buying behavior. Such data depth in connection with the direct accessibility of each target group has never happened before in the history of advertising.

---

[26] Smith, Steve (2012): Fighting The Luma Chart: Criteo's Greg Coleman Lets The Numbers Do The Talking, published 15.06.2012 in Mediapost.com, URL: http://www.mediapost.com/publications/article/176904/fighting-the-luma-chart-criteos-greg-coleman-let.html?print#axzz2KXsTODkU, Stand: 10.07.2013

The self-defining target group

Which revolutionary force works behind the possibilities of Facebook becomes clear when one considers the process of planning an advertising campaign in more detail. In classic media planning, first is the definition of a target group for a specific product focus. The delimitation of these groups will be based on age, gender, income, or education level. If a marketer has defined its target audience for a given product, the entire brand communication can be adjusted accordingly.

For the advertising and media planning, this means that many advertising media such as newspapers, magazines, and television broadcasts need to prove their corresponding user communities and their own target groups. All traditional media companies state in their media kits what audiences and sinus milieus can be reached through their publications.

But this target group approach also has weaknesses. Because whether the assessment of the potential target group actually coincides with the buying public is never guaranteed.

Campaign optimization based on the user reaction in real time

Unlike on Facebook, because of the return channel, the direct user response can now be included in campaign planning. Instead of determining the target groups before, they define themselves during the campaign. How this new type of campaign planning in practice might look like shows a case study from the media-planning agency Efficient Frontier, as the example of the advertiser Urbantrendsetter, an online store for trendy fashion brands.[27] The planners initially switched on a test budget on Facebook without special restriction on targeting groups. Then they evaluated the test results. It was found that mainly women of ages between 40 and 46 years

---

[27] Byza, Christian (2012): Efficient Frontier Case Study, Key Note d3con Conference, Hamburg, Germany

responded to the advertising next to the presumed younger target group. It was also clear that the number of clicks and the subsequent sales 6:00 p.m. to 21:00 clock was particularly high. Even more surprising: people who had liked *Star Wars* likely ordered something in the urban trendsetter online shop. Based on these results, the planning data of the subsequent large-scale campaign has been adjusted. Thus the cost per sale during the campaign could be reduced by almost 50 percent.

Social targeting as a new dimension

The targeting of individual users is only one way to optimize advertising campaigns on Facebook. In addition, there is the possibility to involve a degree of social relation into the targeting. For example, the friends of fans or brand can be explicitly addressed. The effect is not only the behavior of the individual, but also social relations and behaviors within groups, milieu, and target groups can be considered in planning of the campaign.

The depth of data offered to the advertisers for accurate targeting of their campaigns on Facebook is the key to success. Facebook now has over 500 targeting criteria and partnerships with the largest data providers in the United States such as Acxiom and Datalogix Epsilon in addition to enriching Facebook's own treasure trove of data.[28] Also the use of external data through re-targeting technologies is possible since the introduction of the Facebook Ad Exchange in late 2012.

Facebook copies the Google ad system

Looking for the recipe for success of Facebook, you quickly end up back at the Google model. Even Mark Zuckerberg and

---

[28] Peterson, Tim (2013): Facebook Opens Up Ad Targeting to Minivan-Driving, Baby Food-Buying Homemakers, published on 10.04.2013 in Adweek, URL: http://www.adweek.com/news/technology/facebook-opens-ad-targeting-minivan-driving-baby-food-buying-homemakers-148500, Date 10.07.2013

his team focused on the development of the platform from a user point of view. Initially, the focus was on the development of skillful features such as the news feed with all activities of a user's Facebook friends for constantly new content and changes on the Facebook homepage of each user. With the ability to tag people in photos, the interaction of the members among themselves further increased. Facebook could ultimately prevail against competitors such as Tribester, Google's Orkut, Friendster, or Myspace, all of which stand for earlier, nonviable precursors of the evolutionary path of social networks. Only when the competition was out of the way, Facebook made the next step and thought about how to monetize the resounding success among users.

To build up its promotional offer, Facebook ensured support by competent authorities: in March 2008, Zuckerberg appointed Sheryl Sandberg as chief operating officer of Facebook. Sandberg had previously been responsible for the whole Google ad sales business as vice president of global online sales and operations at Google. She made sure that Facebook's advertising model was based on the same basic pillars, which had also helped Google's breakthrough. Not surprisingly, the Facebook advertising model is based on the same business logic:

- ✓ **Risk split for advertisers** *through performance-based pricing* **on click basis**
- ✓
- ✓ **Auction-based price modeling**

- ✓ **Data-driven delivery of the ads**

The sales figures of Facebook are so far impressive and reminiscent of the early success of Google. Both companies brought it in the fourth year after the start of their advertising activity each to just under $4 billion in sales. The financial figures speak for themselves: in 2011, Facebook and Google each had a margin of around 27 percent, sales per employee was US$1.17 versus US$1.16 million at approximately the same level. The profit per employee was with US$310,000 at Facebook even just over the approximately US$300,000 from Google.[29]

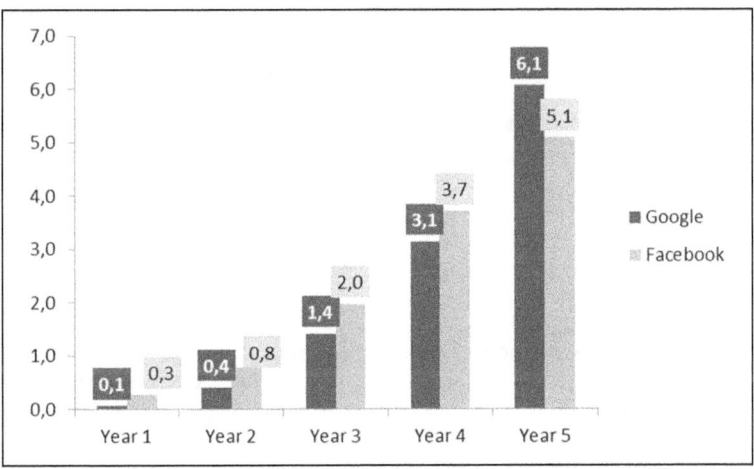

Figure 15: Advertising revenues of Google and Facebook in the first five years, in billions of US dollars.
(Source: Company data; author illustration)

But in the fifth year of the prodigy, Facebook seemed to weaken. The problem becomes even more evident looking at the sales numbers per user: Facebook earned in 2012 only an average of US$4.5 per user with the sale of advertisements. Google, however, had sales of about $38 per user for the same period.[30] The reason that for the optimization of pure direct sales campaigns to Facebook data pool is much worse than Google search algorithm.

---

[29] Google Annual Report 2012 Annual Report 2012 Facebook, own calculations
[30] Koehn, Stefan (2012): The great Google+ plan, published online on 23.06.2012, URL: http://www.stefan-koehn.de/blog/2012/06/der-google-plus-plan/, as 10.07.2013

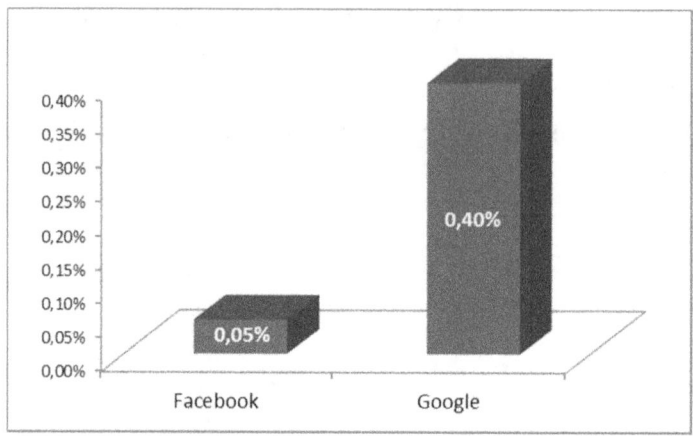

Figure 16: Average Banner Click-Through-Rates Facebook vs. Google 2012.
(Quelle: eMarketer, Webtrends)

While Google users are searching for a product when they use the search engine, Facebook users are not necessarily in the shopping mode. They prefer to click through the status messages and picture galleries of their friends then to pay attention to the small text ads. The average CTR of Facebook banners is at 0.05 percent, far below the average CTR of Google with 0.4 percent.[31]

The technology jump

For Facebook, but also for all other companies that rely on advertising as a business model, this direct sales focus is increasingly becoming a problem. Despite the extremely high range and number of members, Facebook sales are still comparatively low, and the market is still dominated by Google.

---

[31] eMarketer, Webtrends (2012)

Real-time bidding threatened Google's core business

But Google also is under pressure through the development of data-driven advertising in the form of re-targeting and real-time bidding. The company responded in mid-2012 and has adapted its terms and conditions worldwide so that the use of data in the Google universe is possible across all services. Once a user logs into a Google service, Google will begin to create a profile for each user. All searches can now be saved and compressed to anonymous user and search profiles. Google's algorithm now not only shows ads based on specific key words within a search query or the content of the website, but also on the user profile. The new method has been successful: the number of clicks increased by 42 percent in 2012.[32]

However, with the new technical standard for real-time bidding, Google's advertisers can now access advertising inventory on ad exchanges and SSPs independent from Google. With the Amazon Ad Exchange, one of the first of Google's top advertisers has already woken up. The company could suffer considerable losses in a sales-driven budget.

---

[32] Frankfurter Allgemeine Zeitung 2012): More clicks on Google ads can increase sales, published online on 20.07.2012, 10.07.2013, URL http://www.faz.net/aktuell/wirtschaft/internet-mehr-klicks-auf-werbung-lassen-google-umsatz-steigen-11826197.html, date 10.07.2013

Chapter Five: The branding bet

Executive Summary

Until now, the Internet is used primarily for sales-oriented campaigns. But the mechanics of data-driven advertising delivery and performance-based billing also can be applied to the needs of advertisers that today still advertise in print and TV. Once the new competitors such as Google and Facebook manage to adapt the technology of data-driven advertising on the advertising goals of branding advertisers, it could lead to a dramatic shift in this budget. Thus Christensen described that a typical jump with disruptive technologies in the premium market would take place.

Quality content plays a crucial role to this development since the consumption of text or movies brings the user into an appropriate usage situation for pull-marketing actions.

The technology of data-driven advertising has created a new market in the form of Google's search advertising. Databased methods such as the re-targeting model have evolved in this niche market of sales-driven online advertising. Thus, until today, the established media companies were not directly threatened in their core business with high-priced image ads. Following Christensen's theory of disruptive innovations, the technology of the return-channel-based ad delivery will soon move up into the more advanced and higher-margin premium market, and the new competitors are going to attack TV and print companies in their core business.

The advantages of the new technology are evident also for brand advertisers: direct measurability, modulation, and optimization of campaigns in real time and a performance-based billing model, which provides a split of the investment risk between advertiser and media company.

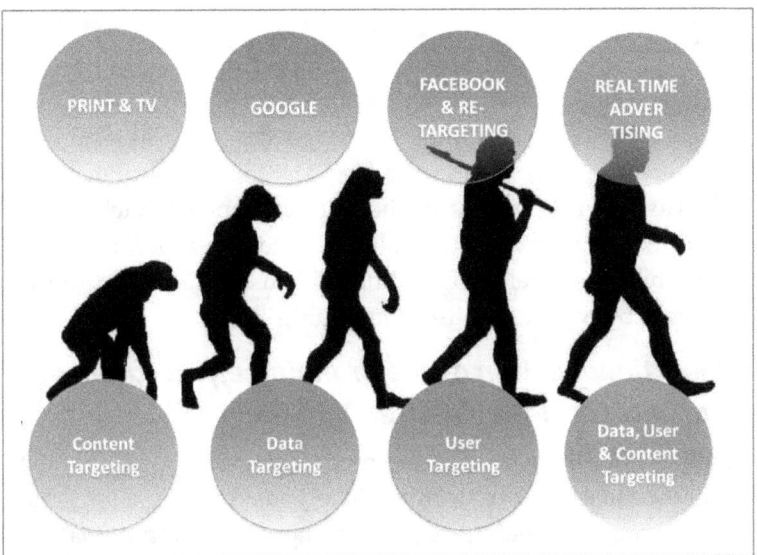

Figure 17: The evolution of data-driven advertising.
(Source: author illustration)

From the perspective of an advertiser, the return-channel-driven advertising is superior to the traditional media in many important respects.

Thus, to transfer the mechanics of the data-driven advertising from the direct sales to the branding business, three important components are required:

✓ *A **real-time measurable index** of the **advertising effectiveness***

✓ ***Appropriate content** and **advertising formats** that allow such advertising success*

✓ ***User data** to increase and guarantee **ad relevance***

In search for the digital branding KPI

A central role for the success of digital content environments as an advertising medium for branding ads plays on the introduction of a uniform proof for the measurement of advertising effectiveness in the digital channels. Such a key performance index (KPI) is also needed for a performance-based billing model for branding advertisement to ensure the risk split between advertisers and publishers.

Operationalization of the branding effect rather than direct sales evidence

Unlike the direct sales-oriented campaigns where the clearance sales are online immediately measurable, there is no way to measure the effect of branding advertising directly— yet. Although the Internet seduces with its wide variety of measurement options and the flood of data to the idea that one could now clarify the effectiveness of advertising to 100 percent, this seems to be a fallacy. For models such as the customer journey, it is more about the question of how a customer converts the purchase decision he has already taken. Thus the data collection plays more in the *purchasing logistics* and not to the actual reasons for the emergence of a purchase decision in the user's brain.

Many products have a very long sales cycle or cannot be ordered online. A car brand wants to create awareness for its brand or arouse certain emotions. Therefore it is necessary to ensure that the advertising and effective format is delivered to the appropriate target group. A direct purchase is not expected here.

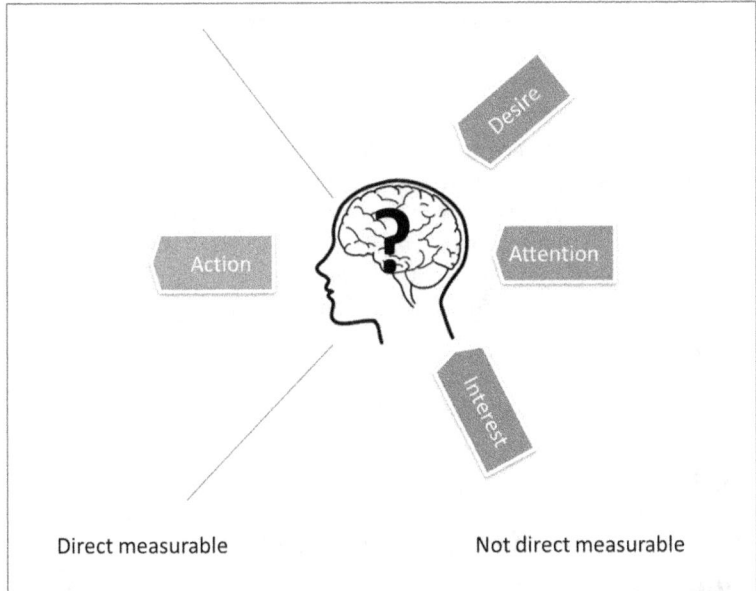

Figure 18: Measurability of the AIDA stages.
(Source: author illustration)

The same goes for the classic pull advertising of fast-moving consumer goods. Here it is just the stimulus that should be activated in a consumer's mind in the hope that he or she also picks the right the supermarket candy bars. What really happens in the brain of a consumer will probably long remain unclear and further contribute to the Wanamaker to 50 percent of wasted advertising expenditures.

Digression: Advertising and advertising effectiveness

"Half the money I spend on advertising is wasted; the trouble is I don't know which half."

John Wanamaker (*July 11, 1838), American businessman and former Postmaster General of the United States

The oft-cited quote of the American businessman and father of modern advertising is still up to date, despite numerous attempts to produce a scientific and clearly demonstrable causal relationship between advertising and advertising effectiveness. This is due to the complexity of the process of inclusion of advertisements in the human brain and in the many stimulus faults we received during the reception of an advertising message alongside. However, no one can doubt that advertising works. After Wanamaker, 50 percent of advertising spending money is well spent; the rest goes to unavoidable handling costs. So the study of cause-and-effect principles of advertising effectiveness is no longer in the foreground for advertisers and media companies. It is about the operationalization of the functioning units of advertising.

Google and Facebook are working hard on such a branding KPI that could be similar to the gross rating points (GRP) model in TV advertising.

Quality contents are the key to branding budgets

In addition to a uniform measurement of advertising effectiveness, high-quality content in the form of journalistic articles, reports, and broadcasting formats such as movies and television series play a crucial role in the transfer of branding budgets to digital channels. A resolution of GroupM highlights the importance of high-quality content as a significant advertising environment. The world's second largest communications holding company, WPP owned media agency, announced in 2011 to invest only in legitimate, professionally produced advertising environments, as advertisers rely on a high-quality content environment for the staging of their brands. [33]

Here Google and Facebook have one major drawback. Unlike traditional media companies, Google does not provide its reach through high-quality content, but through technological

---

[33] Morrissey, Brian (2012): Where GroupM Sees Digital Going, erschienen online in didgday am 29.11.2012, URL: http://www.digiday.com/agencies/where-groupm-sees-digital-going/, Stand 10.07.2013

platforms, which are filled with through algorithms or with user-generated content. The consequences for the sale of advertising in such an environment show the example of video advertising. In the United States, the advertising revenues that could be redeemed with professionally produced content are at the same level as the sales of the two largest video platforms, Vimeo and YouTube. [34]

Content Quality	Content Providers		Estimated market volume in Million US $ 2012
Made for Broadcast	itv	vevo TV ESPN NYT Digital	800-1.200
	Wall Street Journal Digital	MSNBC	
Made for Digital	Yahoo! YouTube Pro Channels	AOL blinkx	100-200
User Generated	Youtube	Vimeo	900-1.100

Figure 19: Estimated market volume of advertising revenues for video content in the United States.
(Source: McKinsey, Dr. Marcus Frerker, Horizon Media Congress 2013, customized appearance)

Although Vimeo and YouTube have multiple reach of the classical broadcaster online, the difference is that the video from Vimeo and Google platforms are primarily filled with user-generated content and are therefore unsuitable as advertising environments. This development shows that in addition to the direct proof of the branding advertising performance, quality content plays a central role in the development of branding budgets online. And here the

---

[34] Frerker, Dr. Marcus (2013): "everything everywhere – What consumers want and what media companies need to adapt," McKinsey presentation on the Horizont Media Congress 2013, Frankfurt, Germany

established media companies still hold an important trump card.

High user engagement prevents pull-advertising reception

In addition to the preferences of advertisers, there is another reason why the type of content has a central role in the shift of branding budgets to digital channels. Text and moving image content, in which a story is told, establishes the recipient in a lean-back situation. Here the seductive power of advertising can take full effect. Well-made advertising can also fulfill the need of the user for distraction as well as the content itself. And only in such a receiving mode is pull advertising possible without disturbing the user.

Digression: Pull and push marketing

When it comes to **pull marketing**, the advertising goal is to stimulate demand for a product at the customer very early in the decision process. Classically, this marketing form is used to address the first three stages of the AIDA: attention, interest, and desire. Appropriate advertising bookings and campaigns are carried out in TV and print media, since they achieve high coverage at relatively low cost and keep the user in a lean-back position, which is needed for this kind of advertising.

Push marketing is trying to animate a customer who has already made a general decision to buy a particular product. This mostly happens right at the point of sale in the form of discounts or best-price promotions. As the Internet has evolved through the success of online shopping to a gigantic point-of-sale, it dominates previously advertising push.

In such a *lean-back* modus, the user is open to commercial messages, even though he is not necessarily interested in a product in this moment. In contrast, online search or the time spent online surfing a social network is related with high user engagement. Pull advertising that starts early in the AIDA model to stimulate demand for a product by a consumer is to be perceived in the context of search-engine advertising and social networks as extremely disturbing.

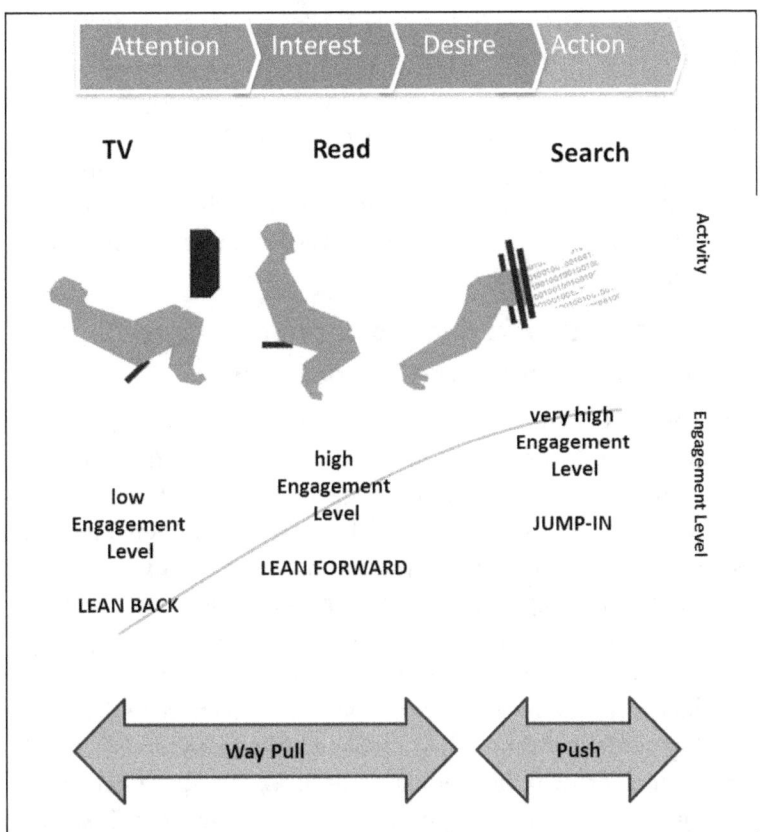

Figure 20: Situation and use of appropriate forms of advertising.
(Source: based on TrendOne; author illustration)

Large-format advertising is not accepted at all by the users on the Google search engine. Google had cancelled a promotion for personalizing the home page of its search engine. Many users appeared irritated because the Google home page was only available with a full-page ad in the background for Google's new service. The planned promotion for 24 hours was therefore stopped after only 14 hours. Marissa Mayer, at that time vice president for search products at Google, tweeted "Google background from tomorrow back to normal."[35]

---

[35] Sawall, Achim (2010): Google published Golem.de, URL: http://www.golem.de/1006/75730.html, Stand 10.07.2013

The same is true for Facebook. The network has increasing difficulties in integrating the advertising messages of the advertisers in its own platform in a way that users do not perceive advertising as too disruptive. Especially with the very personal information that provides the newsfeed of friends and acquaintances, the advertising display is easily interpreted as an invasion of privacy.

External Networks and professional produced contents: Extending the combat zone

However, Google and Facebook are both looking for a solution to the content problem. Google necessarily wants to offer advertisers who still do image advertisements in TV and print channels the ability to place their commercials and advertisements online in premium content environments using the Google platform. Therefore the technology provider Admeld was acquired in 2011 to get access to high-quality content from the renowned media company and be able to display large advertising formats in conjunction with high-quality content. Admeld had managed to win a who-is-who of traditional print publishers such as IDG, Tribune Company, Gannett Co., Hearst Corporation, or the *New York Times* as their clients. This client list was worth at least over $400 million to Google. To also offer high-quality video content as an environment for commercials, Google had its YouTube managers drive through their main markets in the United States and Europe and contract with national TV production companies.

According to insiders, Facebook also has long been working on an external network, through which large-format advertising can be delivered outside its own platform in premium environments based on Facebook user data. Therefore in 2010 Facebook has committed another Google top manager: Gokul Rajaram, inventor of the Google AdSense program. [36] With the acquisition of the ad server technology provider Altas in March 2013 from Microsoft, Facebook made an additional important step in the direction of its own advertising network.

User data: The fight for the Cookie

With the social plug-in from Facebook, millions of websites today already have implemented a small code snippet that could allow Facebook to deliver ads outside the Facebook platform in the future and to collect additional user data. Originally, the website owners had this plug-in installed so that their users can easily post articles and content on Facebook. The idea: more traffic on its own web pages. However, the principle will also work in the opposite direction. Facebook can use the plug-ins to identify its users on third-party websites and collect data.

In addition to its search engine, Google has brought a number of other products on the market to increase the number of touch points with its users. The business model of some of these services might not be clear at a first glance. But all of Google's offerings are managed centrally via one login—and Google does not log out anyone. Anyone who has ever logged into a Google service has as long-time identification cookie on his or her device and remains identifiable until that person actively logs out—but very few do.

Thus with Google and Facebook, the two largest data collectors in the online world, users can constantly refine their user profiles and get better in adapting their advertising to the current situation and needs of their users

---

[36] Carlson, Nicholas (2012): Facebook's $100 Billion Valuation Pretty Much Depends On This One Guy, published online in Business Insider 14.02.2012, URL: http://articles.businessinsider.com/2012-02-14/tech/31057835_1_facebook-adsense-text-ads , Stand 10.07.2013

Besides Google and Facebook, companies such as Yahoo and Twitter offer so-called social login services. Website operators have the opportunity to simplify their registration process by identifying users through their social media accounts.

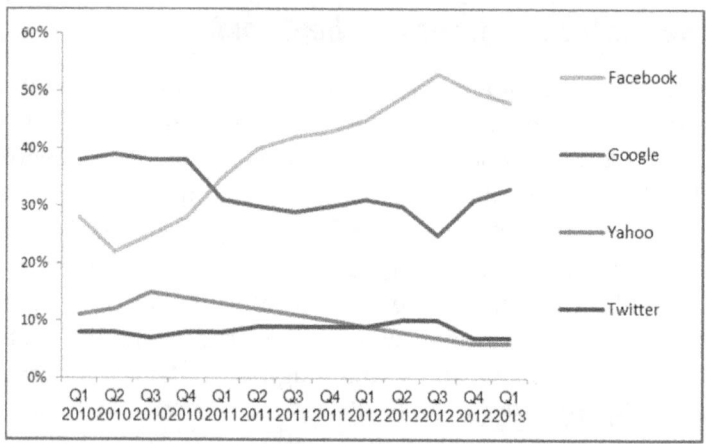

Figure 21: Market share of social logins to log into third-party websites.
(Quelle: Jainrain 2013, US market share, own illustration)

The service is often used especially of e-commerce stores, as here a simple registration process means money. At the same time, the login operator generates valuable data on the purchasing behavior of individual users.

Chapter Six: Technology hype cycle and the login effect

Executive Summary

Instead of adapting the new technologies, many traditional media companies proceed in the evolutionary development of their existing print and TV offerings, even though this strategy poses great risks, according to Clayton Christensen. They run into the risk to miss the adaptation of the new technology in the form of data-driven advertising. Here, another typical pattern in terms of technological innovation appears: "technology hype cycle."

Technological innovations often develop in cycles. There is a curve that is described as "technology hype cycle." When introducing a technical innovation, the first hype is often followed by disappointment, as the technology cannot immediately meet the high expectations. Therefore the technological maturity needs to first develop into a niche market. It also speaks of the "chasm," a term Geoffrey A. Moore coined in his 1991 book *Crossing the Chasm.*[37]

"The Chasm represents a gap between the Early Market and the next phase: the Bowling Alley. It develops when there are few if any remaining visionaries to sell to but pragmatists are not yet ready to adopt. Pragmatists do not see a complete solution to their problem, plus there is no group of references that have formed that they trust. In addition, they want to see the solution working live at customer sites. Revenue growth ceases or even recedes in the Chasm. The length of this market lull is uncertain."

---

[37] Moore, Geoffrey A. (1991): Crossing the Chasm, New York

Data-driven advertising and the technology hype cycle

Many companies are turning away in this phase disappointed by the new technologies. But these are evolving and as soon as their development curve allows, they do a market shift upward from a niche into the premium market.

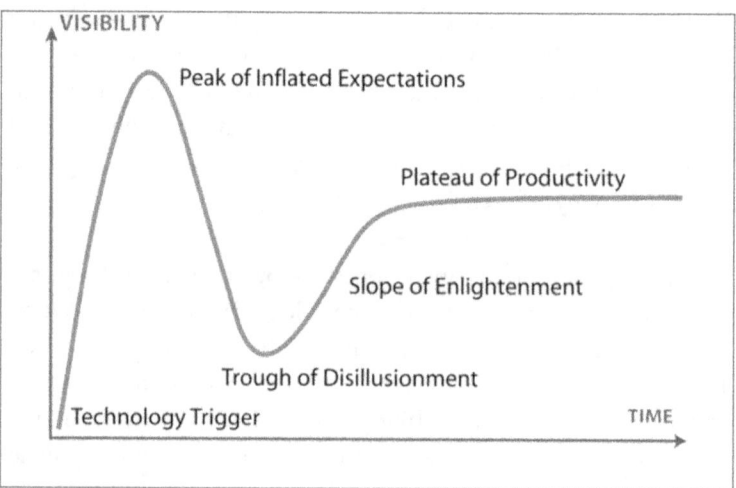

Figure 22: Technology hype cycle by Gartner.
(Source: Gartner Group)

This model can also be applied to the current situation in the media markets. While many publishers turn away disappointed from the marketing opportunities of digital content, TV marketers are optimistic about their digital future. With their video advertising format, they are obviously just at the beginning of such a hype cycle. Their TV commercials seem to work very well online: moving image content is easily transferable and leads to strong user engagement; click-through rates for online video advertising are significantly higher in comparison to the display banner ads. This corresponds to the wishes of advertisers: they love measurable performance metrics.

Due to the good performance results, a real run was triggered on online video advertising in premium environments.

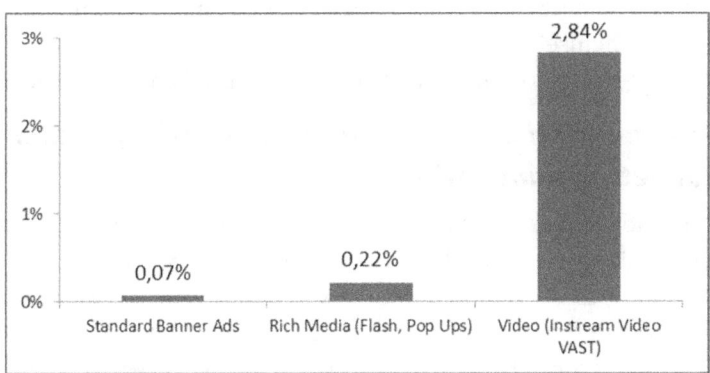

Figure 23: Click-through rates of various online ad formats.
(Source: Mediamind 2012,Eyeblaster, 2012; author illustration)

But the private TV stations opened their archives only gradually. This artificial shortage has two reasons: first, it ensures the high prices for TV stations in the online business. Second, they protect their traditional TV broadcasting business. A true adaptation of new technologies does not take place. None of the digital TV publishers rely on a performance-based pricing model for branding campaigns or make use of data to ensure highly relevant advertising delivery to the user. As with print publishers, the TV distribution model from the back gapless television business is transferred to the new medium. Like this, the television executives are in danger of falling into the same innovation trap as their print counterparts did before.

What goes up can't go down

From the perspective of traditional media companies, it makes no sense simply to venture into an uncertain market environment in which margins are low, earnings and market outlook uncertain, and volumes are still very small compared to the traditional markets in print and TV.

Rather than get involved in the adaption of the new technologies to gain valuable experience in dealing with the disruptive technologies, the established media companies limited themselves to the defense of their own sinecures and to expansion into stagnant or declining market environments.

Prisoners of their own customers: Branding further budgets in print and TV

The adverting clients confirm the established media companies in their behavior. They are accepting new technologies as critical until they can provide the required services; here the generation of advertising effect is cheaper and more efficient—and so far it is not yet. This becomes clear if one considers the allocation of advertising budgets of major industries. The lion's share of branding budgets goes further into the classic offline advertising channels.

Print and especially TV continue to be the preferred media channels among the media agencies and advertisers and are assigned to the high-priced booking for image ads while online bobs on a low level and is mostly recognized as an experimental field or marketing laboratory than as a serious and reliable media channel.

Organizational structure stifles innovation

As in the Christensen model, neither the traditional companies nor their customers drive innovation. The necessary drive and organizational ability are usually only with the new competitors who enter the field from outside markets and make use of the disruptive technologies.

According to Christensen, the reason for this lies in the organizational structure of the established companies. And here you can see again a parallel to the current situation of the media companies: most sales units for the digital offerings of publishers and television stations are in the reporting line of the print and TV divisions. As a result, they are more likely to be agents of the established models as to be drivers of innovation within the corporate organization because TV and print marketers have not internalized into their organizational DNA to primarily promoting new distribution channels, but to protect their existing business. This also becomes evident when looking at the motivation of the individual market participants.

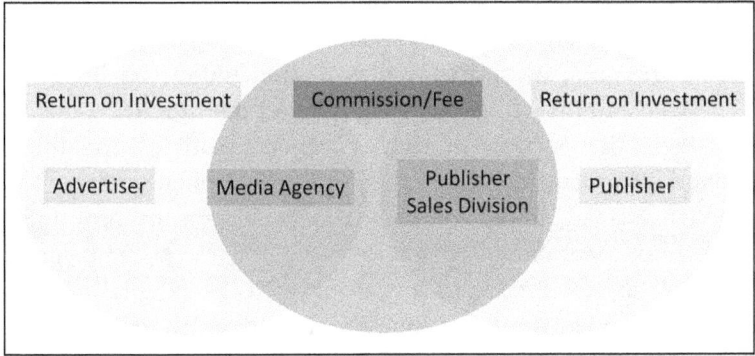

Figure 24: Overlap of the spheres of interest of marketers and media agency.
(Source: author illustration)

It comes to a clear overlap between the spheres of interest in various areas. Above all, through their commission-based earning model, publisher's sales units and advertiser's media agencies are more motivated on maintaining the status quo of the established system rather than to promote innovations.

Chapter Seven: How to overcome disruptive challenges in the media market

Executive Summary

In order to overcome the disruptive challenges, the established media companies should strongly reflect back on their core business and adapt new marketing technologies. Above all, the print publishers are faced with tremendous challenges. They have to invest in both the quality of their digital content as well as in the translation of compatible branding advertising formats. Next to that, it is absolutely necessary for the established media companies to develop a uniform and directly measurable performance index for image campaigns on their digital offerings. Only if they sell their digital media on a performance-based billing model and so take account of the return channel, a transfer of branding budgets will succeed.

Christensen shows in his model not only problems, he also offers alternatives. Although it is exceptionally difficult for established companies to cope with disruptive challenges in the form of new technologies, they are not helpless. First of all, Christensen breaks a lance for the manager of incumbents. "Perhaps the most important result of this research project is that poor management can be excluded as an explanation for the failure of established firms."[38] All the things that companies and managers successfully do in *normal markets*, if disruptive innovations occur, surprisingly they guide to failure. Strong customer orientation, careful observation of the competition, investments to improve the efficiency of its products and technologies, growth and margin guidance:

---

[38] Christensen, Clayton S (1997): The Innovators Dilemma, S. 125ff.

these decades' valid recipes for success were suddenly astray, says Christensen.

Spin-off of independent units

The separation of the divisions within the organizational structure of the company is due to Christensen's model an important prerequisite for the success dealing with disruptive challenges and are probably the most difficult to be implemented. Nevertheless, media managers should keep in mind that there is an organizational form needed in which the digital units are no appendages of the traditional offerings. These units must be able to act independently from the core business to adapt to disruptive technologies.

At first glance, most media companies have exactly already followed this strategy. With the introduction of the Internet in the late 1990s, they started out as new digital daughters and turned them formally into independent organizational units, mostly in the form of limited liability companies. The problem is that ultimately the new organizational units still lay in the reporting lines of the managers, who are also responsible for the core business. They had to follow the same rules and criteria making money as the established corporate sectors. And when the quick success failed and further investment would have been necessary, the new drivers of innovation were quickly reincorporated. Although there are some successful examples of such companies near spin-offs, in the emergence of disruptive technologies, it is extremely difficult for the company to protect the new units from the influence of existing business—especially since their attacks threaten the individual spheres of influence leading managers from the core business.

Conscious cannibalization of its core business

The most important step toward addressing disruptive challenges is the active cannibalization of its own core business. Behind it lies a simple idea: as new technologies threaten the existing core business, it is best for established companies when they hold these technologies and virtually cannibalize themself. In this case, that means mainly for publishers first to invest heavily in the quality of their digital offerings, rather than continuing to operate the continuance of their core business.

Investment in the quality of digital content

Especially for publishers, it is important to reclaim their core competency: the creation and marketing of high-quality content. In this area, they have their strengths and have a huge edge in experience, which they should not simply give away after the first deceptive experience with the new medium of the Internet. Content has their place in the digital world and can be refinanced on the sale of high-priced display image— only the quality has to be right.

Arouse desires among users and advertisers

Digital content must be produced so that it provides an added value on top of future print product. Publishers will need to turn into multimedia production houses. Investigative stories and unique journalistic pieces, enriched with additional material and animations, producing complex reports and video material, inspiring the user through the programming of linear content streams similar to those of television—these are the tasks of an editorial in a digitized world.

To ensure such quality, the imbalance within the newsrooms needs to be resolved: the print colleagues have not only been paid better, they also have more time and larger budgets to research their stories. It is not surprising that the best employees continue to be oriented toward print. In the ideal case, it would be more attractive to the best journalists in the future to work for the online editions: they are faster because they have more money and because there are more opportunities there.

The danger of a free event

Only with the corresponding value in the form of elaborately produced journalistic content can users are persuaded to pay for digital editions. A successful monetization of digital content works thus only through quality—if digital editions of newspapers and magazines do not offer an added value on top the print editions, users are not willing to pay for content on the net. Accordingly, all efforts to introduce paid-content models have failed. Giving digitized print content online for free lets the user replace the print editions and save their money at the newsstand.

Digression: The digital dilemma of the New York Times

How difficult the introduction of a pay wall for digitized print content is, shows an example of the *New York Times*. The newspaper veteran did manage to win over 566,000 paying online subscribers by the end of 2012.[39] But the dream of success seems to pop back quickly, even for the *New York Times*. After initial reports of success, the number of online subscribers began to stagnate since mid-2013.

Much more serious: digital subscriber sales generated in 2012 only US$91 million in revenue. So they did, despite the high number of subscribers of only about 12 percent of the total subscription revenues of US$768 million. The reason? While an average print subscriber pays US$730 per year, the high number of digital subscriptions could only be achieved with a much lower subscription price of US$220.[40] The question remains whether it is possible to pay real quality journalism of such low amounts.

---

[39] Kafka, Peter (2012): The New York Times Reports a Digital Success Story, published online in AllthingD on 06.08.2012, URL: http://allthingsd.com/20120806/the-new-york-times-reports-a-digital-success-story/, Date 10.07.2013

[40] Lee, Edmund (2012): The New York Times Paywall Is Working Better Than Anyone Had Guessed, published online in Bloomberg 20.12.2012, URL: http://go.bloomberg.com/tech-blog/2012-12-20-the-new-york-times-paywall-is-working-better-than-anyone-had-guessed/, Stand 10.07.2013

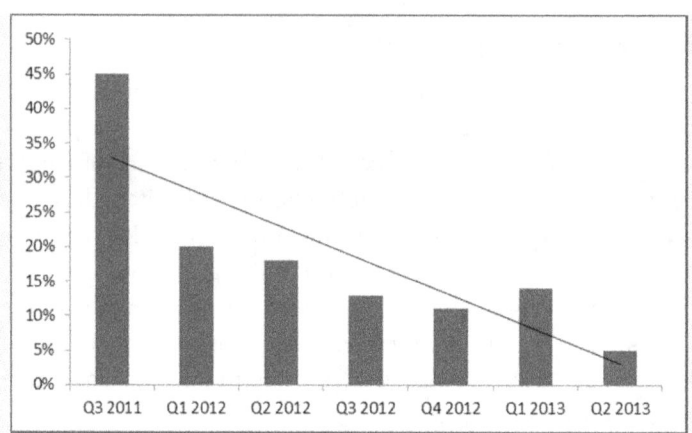

Figure 25: Growth of online subscribers: numbers of the New York Times.
(Source: Company data; author illustration)

Adaptation of the disruptive technologies

The second important step to cope with disruptive challenges is the adaptation of the new technologies. In terms of the monetization of digital, the established media companies need to bridge the gap between the often sold-out home pages and inefficiently used available inventory in the rest. Only when they move onto performance-based pricing models and provide the basis for a data-driven advertising model, the transformation of the core business will succeed. The return channel provides advertisers so many unique advantages that it will lead to a reallocation of budgets in the direction of the digital channels anyhow. Only if established media companies dominate the business with the automated ad trading and data-driven advertising, they ensure they will continue to benefit in the future from the business with the high-priced image ads.

Translation of the branding-compatible ad formats to the digital offerings

Today the most widely used formats such as rectangles or skyscraper ads are completely unsuitable for image campaigns and an anathema for every creative: little boxes, little space, and no room for ideas or special visual creations. No wonder: the standardization of the definition of today's popular banner sizes comes from the year 2000, a time in which a large proportion of users were sitting on small screens using modem Internet access.

While the advertiser receives a 50/50 split between display and text in print, and its advertising message usually stands alone and gets the exclusive attention of the reader on each page, the ads on the digital editions of established media companies are mostly fragmented or interfere with the user experience in the form of annoying pop-up or overlay ads. They are annoying are poorly integrated into the user experience of the website. From the perspective of advertisers, it is an advertising medium that is ignored by the user or bothersome and is a suboptimal form of communication.

Although with wallpaper or homepage takeovers, there are large-format banners in use and are standardized for booking. But these formats are still being sold at fixed prices, which are far above those of TV and print. Thus, large-format banner ads usually occur only on the home pages of the digital offerings.

A general shift to large-format banners that are sold as performance-based would have several advantages. It would automatically lead to a reduction of supply and at the same time improve the performance of the ad.

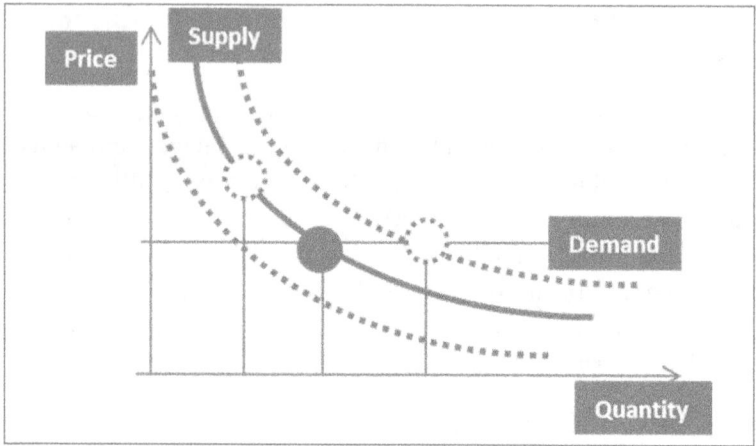

Figure 26: Price elasticity and shift of the demand curve due to a change in the supply.
(Source: author illustration)

Performance-based billing based on KPI

To take account of the return channel, branding campaigns also need to be sold on a performance base in the future. And here we meet an old acquaintance. The click is so far the only measurable quantity of user reaction and an important indicator of whether a campaign has reached its target group. And large ad sizes increase click-through rates. Even today, there are advertisers and media agencies that, despite the refusal of the premium publishers, require a certain minimum numbers of clicks per campaign.

By the potential of increase in click-through rates over larger ad formats with more space for creative ideas in conjunction with the relevant delivery of the advertising banner, the click could work as a basis for a performance-based billing model also for brand advertising.

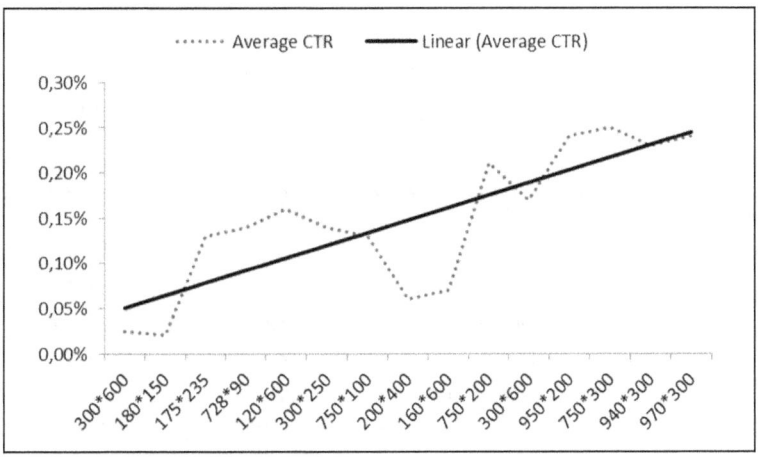

Figure 27: Correlation between click-through rate and banner size.
(Source: IAB Poland in 2012; author illustration)

Click and view time as a uniform branding KPI

A suitable accounting basis for branding campaigns could be a combination of CTR and view time. The advertiser pays only when the advertisement has been delivered for a specific time in the field of view of the user. In conjunction with the click as an additional quality KPI, this could be an efficient and measurable billing model. Ads that are below a predefined CTR must be fixed or replaced by the advertiser. At the same time, both advertising and advertisers are motivated to deliver relevant ads to the user. In this way, the attractiveness of the advertising is guaranteed and prevents media companies from advertisers realizing entrainment effects through ads that, although poorly clicked, are still seen by many users.

Google has already adapted such a model with its "True View" offer for branding campaigns. Advertisers only have to pay for a spot on YouTube if their promotional clip was seen by the user for at least 30 seconds. At the same time, Google also refers the user experience to its deliberations and offers the user the option to skip video ads after the first five seconds or to watch them completely. Costs for the advertiser only arises when users view the video display for at least 30 seconds. That leaves Google and its user-centered product development faithful.

Real-time bidding as digital-advertising operating system

A major disadvantage of the established media companies against new competitors such as Facebook and Google has been the fragmentation of the market into many offers. What, from the perspective of media diversity, seems to be welcomed is a major obstacle for automated ad booking. It would therefore be of great benefit to the national media companies to join forces against the exceedingly powerful attacker from Silicon Valley. This could be the base for a third wide-reaching ad ecosystem alongside Google and Facebook. Real-time bidding could be the operating system for databased ad delivery in high-quality content environments. The real-time bidding process enables targeted and highly relevant ads on the website of established media companies on the basis of any third-party database. The data from Facebook, Google, or the media houses themselves can be used—but also advertisers such as Amazon, eBay, Procter & Gamble, and BMW have access to their own user data to deliver the ads as targeted as possible within the high-quality content contexts of the established media companies.

Recovery of the data equilibrium

A common platform of established media companies would have more advantages: In the digital publishing and TV landscape, it is that currently only media agencies and advertisers can collect user data across different platforms and websites. This creates a classic asymmetry of information for the publishers. The media companies have no insight into the ultimately realized revenues from its inventory and no access to user data. Would they get together and supply user data across all the established media websites, they could offer their own data-driven models. The greater this common platform would be, the more data the company could collect and share to increase advertising relevance to the end user.

A user-based delivery of advertisements could replace the ad impression-based billing, and so it solves the problem of different media currencies in terms of reach and ad delivery. So finally a comparison would be made possible of the advertising service among print, TV, and online media. Also, this assumes a uniform technology platform with the appropriate range. The established media companies would be well advised to think about a common platform on which they themselves have the data ownership of their user base. For this purpose, they must make their inventory accessible for real-time advertising and let the value of each impression be determined by the market, rather than declare a seller's own goods as premium without receiving the corresponding demand.

The ad ecosystem of the future

It is still unclear who will occupy the technological infrastructure and the customer lead to advertising and advertisers for a possible third, automated advertising marketplace outside of Google and Facebook. If the established media companies used their cards right and acted together, they could use the online giants from the United States or defy—because, in addition to the contents of competence, they have another strong pound in the hindquarters: the direct lead to the advertisers and media agencies. Although the media business is becoming an increasingly globalized market, the advertising budgets are still planned and distributed nationally in order to respond to the typical characteristics and tastes of the end users. At this point, the established media companies still have a clear advantage. With the model of private ad exchanges, real-time bidding is a model to be established, dominated by traditional media companies.

Ultimately, it is going to become a question of what is sold in the future to the advertisers: content and strong media brands with the option for the advertiser to use user data from external providers such as Facebook and Google to increase advertising relevance. Or will they take over the lead to the advertisers, automatically process campaign bookings through their platforms, and deliver the ads on the pages of the established media companies?

Chapter Eight: A look into the crystal ball

Executive Summary

The mobile advertising market is growing slowly in comparison to the early years of television and search advertising and is also dominated by Google and Facebook.

Social networks will continue to play an increasingly important role in programming and content, and, through the ongoing convergence of the media markets, there is going to be a clash of digital distribution channels on the home TV screen.

Mobile Internet use is growing rapidly and puts established media companies seemingly under additional pressure. But to understand this development, it is important to distinguish the use of different mobile devices. While tablets are mainly used at home, smartphones are in use on the go. In particular, the use of smartphones distinguishes itself by a particularly high level of commitment and a significant lean-forward experience.

Mobile: The next platform business

This has the consequence that advertising is accepted only when it is highly relevant and promises the highest added value. Through their rich data treasure, Google and Facebook can provide exactly this advertising relevance. They offer advertisers the best performances for their campaigns and therefore dominate the market for mobile advertising.

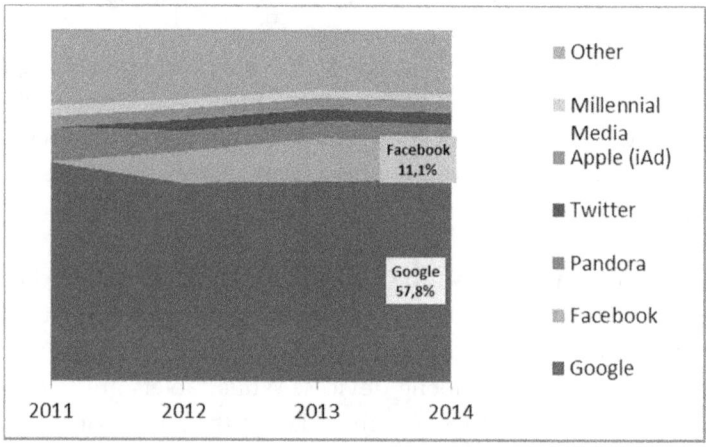

Figure 28: US advertising market share in mobile advertising.
(Source: eMarketer, 2011–1014; author illustration)

For traditional media companies, there is an additional unpleasant feature: brands in the Mobile area are no longer depended on the creation of reach by content providers. They produce own apps that promise users an added value and act as a marketing tool that is much more efficient than the circuit of banners on websites or mobile in-app advertising. Pharmaceutical companies offer interactive allergy calendars to warn the user before pollen and winter sport brands sponsoring powder apps with an alarm for new snow in the user's area. About 90 percent of smartphone traffic takes place not on mobile websites, but within those apps.

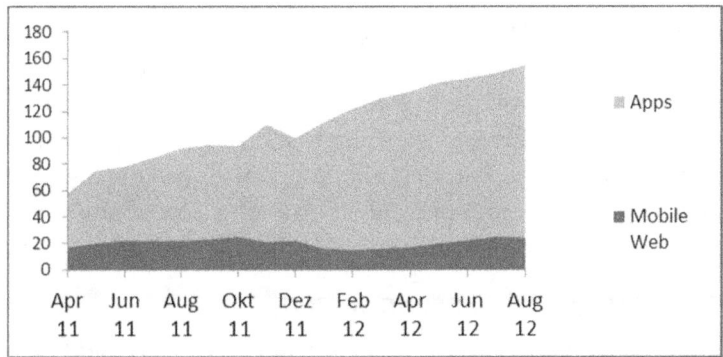

*Figure 29: Use of Internet and apps on iOS and Android
smartphone devices.*
(Source: Business Insider, Nielsen Smartphone Analytiscs, 2013)

All this means that the mobile advertising market is growing much more slowly than other successful advertising channels today after their introduction. Comparing the growth of TV advertising spending or the growth of search advertising market at the beginning of the respective market development, it is clear that the mobile advertising market is clearly *lagging behind.*

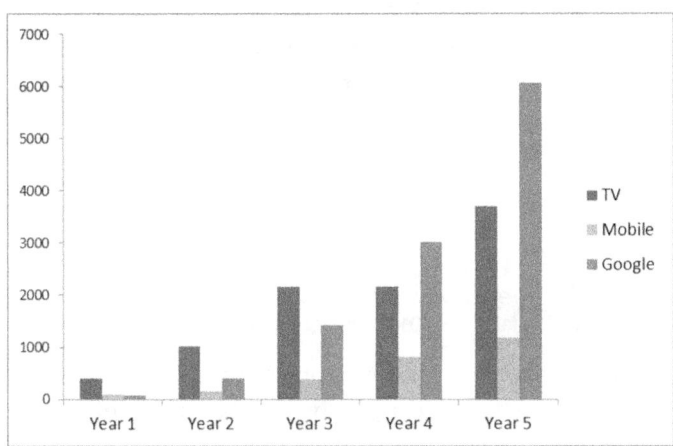

*Figure 30: Growth of individual advertising divisions in the first
five years (U.S. Mobile Ad Spendings vs U.S. TV sales vs.
Google worldwide).*
*(Source: IAB, McKann-Erickson, BIA Kelsey, Business Insider reports,
company information)*

Thus, the mobile advertising on smartphones poses for traditional media companies neither a special endangerment nor great opportunities. Unlike in the tablets, they are mainly used at home or *lean-back* consumption of high-quality content from the user. And here the traditional media companies can score when they prepare their content accordingly and manage to keep the ad sales leaned in their own hands.

Wandering path "second screen"

The debate about the "second screen," the use of PC and tablet parallel to television watching is an aberration for TV sales houses, although digital development departments are popping up with new ideas for interactive concepts for greater involvement of the audience in the program in the form of apps and spectators forums.

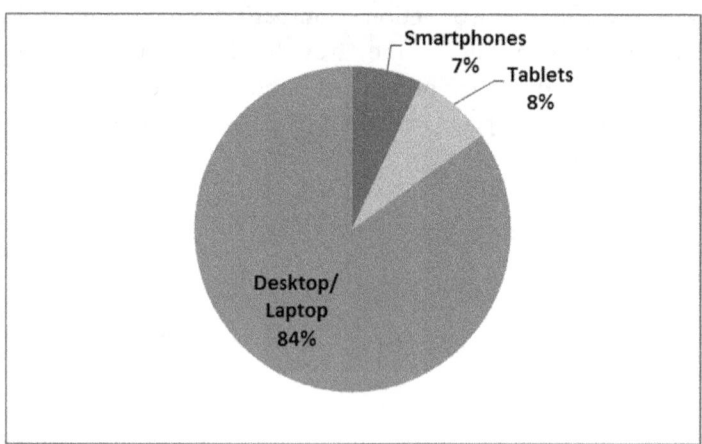

Figure 31: Internet use by device 2013.
(Source: Adobe Digital Index 2013; author illustration)

But this interactivity contradicts one of the main arguments of television managers for the survival of their medium. Because it completely breaks with the linear narrative form of television—whichever lets you switch off after work. And only in this lean-back situation, the user is willing to accept pull-advertising messages as part of the entertainment. Moreover, all the communication and interaction on the *second screen* is based on an event that takes place on the *first screen*, the TV screen, and is easy to reach for advertisers.

At the same time, TV marketers are facing the same problems as with their online sales: it requires uniform indicators to measure advertising effectiveness and performance-based pricing models. Next to that, very often, communication about a television event takes place not within the apps the TV channel offers, but within the social networks such as Twitter or Facebook, in which there is no chance to sell advertising at all for the TV channels on this platforms.

TV: The replacement of the gatekeeper

If one understands the programming of content in addition to advertising sales as the core competence of a TV station, the biggest challenge is the inclusion of media-usage behavior into the programming of personalized content streams.

Facebook as program director

The inclusion of social networks, however, plays a crucial role. The social network relationships enable a more accurate selection of potentially interesting content. The media behavior of individuals can be clustered in order to adapt the content programming. The data on the media-consumption habits of Facebook friends helps to find the most interesting content for each individual user. Thus the gatekeeper function of program editors resolves: linear television will only function accompanying to the personalized program window in the future. What sounds like the distant future is already reality. YouTube allows its users to link their own Facebook profile with a YouTube account. In an extra-social channel-only content that has been seen by Facebook friends will be displayed. Now suggestions are mostly for music videos and user-generated content. But once you replace this content mentally by an American HBO series, high-quality documentaries or feature films, the potential of this innovation becomes clear.

Whether the private television will survive the digital transformation processes in the long run or not remains to be seen. If it were up to the philosopher David Precht, it would not even be pity for it. In an interview with the online magazine *Carta*, he said the private television lacks from any social benefit.[41] The commercial television was only created to make money. The social function of education, bringing together people about the setting of priorities, however, is the task of public service broadcasters and, last but not least, the newspaper and magazine publishers.

Seen like this, the publishers have a social responsibility not to fail because of the digital challenges. It is time for publishers to meet their journalistic responsibilities in a digitized world again, act more enterprising and courageous, and don't let their journalistic work be dictated by their sales organizations. The chances for that are good. Newspapers and magazines are a haptical experience and therefore not 100 percent digitalizable. They can survive with higher copy prices and even without advertising—perhaps even more critical, with more independence and more quality.

---

[41] Precht, Richard David (2010): "Die Gesellschaft braucht das Privatfernsehen nicht", online erschienen am CARTA am 13.12.2010, URL: http://carta.info/35058/precht-die-gesellschaft-braucht-das-privatfernsehen-nicht/, Stand 10.07.2013

Bibliography
Used and further reading

Chapman, Merrill R. (2006): In Search of Stupidity – Over 20 Years of High-Tech Marketing Disasters, New York

Christensen, Clayton M. (1997): The innovator's dilemma: when new technologies cause great firms to fail, Boston, Massachusetts, USA

Dumitrescu, Delia (2011): Road Trip to Innovation – How I came to understand Future Thinking, Hamburg

Levine, Robert (2011): Free Ride, New York

Levy, Steven (2012): Google Inside, New York

Lumann, Niklas (2004): Die Realität der Massenmedien, München

MacFarquhar. Larissa (2000): The New Gilded Age edited by David Remnick, New York

McQuivey, James (2013): Digital Disruption, Las Vegas

Moore, Geoffrey A (1991): Crossing the Chasm, New York

Riepl, Wolfgang (1913): Das Nachrichtenwesen des Altertums mit besonderer Rücksicht auf die Römer, Heidelberg

Dossiers & White Papers

Abraham, Magid (2012): The Economics of Advertising, ComScore, San Francisco

Bulow, Nicolas von (2012): Clipperton Ad-Tech White Paper, Paris

Distinguin, Stéphane (2011): Amazon.com: the Hidden Empire, Paris

Benway, J. P. (1998). Banner blindness: The irony of attention grabbing on the World Wide Web. Proceedings of the Human Factors and Ergonomics Society 42nd Annual Meeting, 1, 463-467.

Editorials

B. J. Fogg, J. Marshall, O. Laraki u. a. (2001): What Makes Web Sites Credible? A Report on a Large Quantitative Study Persuasive Technology Lab, Stanford University

Hilbert, Martin/López, Priscila (2011): The World's Technological Capacity to Store, Communicate, and Compute Information, Science, 332 (6025), S. 60-65

Kim, Larry (2012): Google vs. Facebook, Wordstream Studie, URL: http://www.wordstream.com/facebook-vs-google Stand 10.07.2013

Kondratieff, Nikolai D. (1926): Die langen Wellen der Konjunktur, in: Archiv für Sozialwissenschaft und Sozialpolitik

M. Burke, A. Hornof, E. Nilsen, N. Gorman (2004): High-Cost Banner Blindness: Ads Increase Perceived Workload, Hinder Visual Search, and Are Forgotten

St. Elmo Lewis, E (1903): "Catch-Line and Argument." In: The Book-Keeper, Vol. 15

Press Articles

Adexchanger (2011): CEO Mouzykantskii Says IPONWEB Expanding Media Trading Tech Business Globall, published in Adexchanger 05.12.2011, URL: http://www.adexchanger.com/online-advertising/iponweb/, Stand 10.07.2013

Carlson, Nicholas (2012): Facebook's $100 Billion Valuation Pretty Much Depends On This One Guy, published online in Business Insider 14.02.2012, URL: http://articles.businessinsider.com/2012-02-14/tech/31057835_1_facebook-adsense-text-ads, Stand 10.07.2013

D'Angelo, Frank (2009): Happy Birthday, Digital Advertising! – The Banner Campaign that Started a $24 billion Business, and Got a 78 % Click-through Rate, published 26.10 2009 online in Adage, URL: http://adage.com/digitalnext/post?article_id=139964, Stand 10.07.2013

Farber, Dan (2013): Amazon Studios debuts 14 pilots for free viewing, URL: http://news.cnet.com/8301-1023_3-57580146-93/amazon-studios-debuts-14-pilots-for-free-viewing

Forbes Magazine (2011): "Gordon Moore," URL: http://www.forbes.com/profile/gordon-moore/

Internet Pioneers (2010) Portrait Robert Metcalfe, URL: http://www.ibiblio.org/pioneers/metcalfe.html

Hilbert, Martin/López, Priscila (2011): The World's Technological Capacity to Store, Communicate, and Compute Information, Science, 332 (6025), S. 60-65

Kafka, Peter (2012): The New York Times Reports a Digital Success Story, URL: http://allthingsd.com/20120806/the-new-york-times-reports-a-digital-success-story/, Stand 10.07.2013

Lawler, Rayen (2012): Netflix Strikes Streaming Deal With Disney, Gains Exclusive Access To New Titles Beginning In 2016, URL: http://techcrunch.com/2012/12/04/netflix-disney/

Lee, Edmund (2012): The New York Times Paywall Is Working Better Than Anyone Had Guessed, URL: http://go.bloomberg.com/tech-blog/2012-12-20-the-new-york-times-paywall-is-working-better-than-anyone-had-guessed/

Lomas, Natasha (2013): Netflix's 'House Of Cards' Is Internet TV-Funded Original Programming But Don't Kid Yourself It's Ad-Free, URL: http://techcrunch.com/2013/02/11/netflixs-house-of-cards-is-internet-tv-funded-original-programming-but-dont-kid-yourself-its-ad-free-spoiler-alert/

Matyszczyk, Chris (2013): Netflix enjoys fine Kevin Spacey ad at White House dinner, URL: http://news.cnet.com/8301-17852_3-57581791-71/netflix-enjoys-fine-kevin-spacey-ad-at-white-house-dinner/ Stand 10.07.2013

Morrissey, Brian (2012): Where GroupM Sees Digital Going, URL: http://www.digiday.com/agencies/where-groupm-sees-digital-going/

Peterson, Tim (2013): AppNexus's $75 Million Funding Round Quiets Acquisition, IPO Talk, URL: http://www.adweek.com/news/advertising-branding/AppNexus-75-million-funding-round-quiets-acquisition-ipo-talk-146759

Peterson, Tim (2013): Facebook Opens Up Ad Targeting to Minivan-Driving, Baby Food-Buying Homemakers, URL: http://www.adweek.com/news/technology/facebook-opens-ad-targeting-minivan-driving-baby-food-buying-homemakers-148500

Smith, Steve (2012): Fighting The Luma Chart: Criteo's Greg Coleman Lets The Numbers Do The Talking, URL: http://www.mediapost.com/publications/article/176904/fightin g-the-luma-chart-criteos-greg-coleman-let. html?print#axzz2KXsTODkU

About the Author

Nicolas Clasen (born 1974 in Hamburg, Germany) lives and works as an independent business consultant and author in Munich.

During his career, he has always been a frontier runner between established media companies and fast-moving start-ups. Most recently, he supported the technology provider Improve Digital with its rollout in Germany, Austria, and Switzerland.

Nicolas Clasen has a degree in economics and has studied economics at the University of Witten/Herdecke. He is involved in the Federal Association of the Digital Economy (BVDW), and there he was co-initiator of the real-time advertising labs, a professional group-wide initiative on real-time advertising.

For more information on the Internet, please visit

www.digicas.de/en

Stocks

A Newbies' Guide

An Everyday Guide to the Stock Market

Alan Northcott

www.alannorthcott.com

www.newbiesguidetostocks.com

Copyright Notice

First Printing, 2013

ISBN-13: 978-1492998525

ISBN-10: 1492998524

Printed in the United States of America

Contents

Disclaimer and Risk Disclosure 1

Introduction..3

What is a Stock? 5

Market Sectors 7

Company Size 7

Going Public 8

What to Expect 10

Types of Holding 11

Stocks vs. Other Investments................. 13

Mutual Funds.. 14

Other Funds 16

Managed Accounts...................................... 16

Savings Accounts 17

Property Investment 17

Crowd Funding 18

Summary... 19

How the Stock Market Works 21

Stock dealings... 22

Stock Splits... 23

Delisting 24

Share Options 24

Takeovers.. 25

Bankruptcy 26

Why a Stock Price Changes 29

Supply and Demand 29

Making Money... 31

Estimating Worth 32

Does Analysis Work? 33

Types of Analysis............................ 34

Doing The Numbers............................ **37**

P/E Ratio............................ 38

P/S Ratio............................ 39

P/B Ratio 40

Debt Ratio 40

Sources of Information 41

Looking at Charts............................ **47**

What Is A Trend? 48

What Strategies Can You Use?............... **53**

Simplest First 54

Momentum............................ 55

What about Dividends?............................ 56

Looking for Growth............................ 57

Finding a Value 59

Gaining From Splits............................ 60

Insider Buying............................ 62

The Answer? 63

Now Practice............................ 65

How to Make Your Trades............... **71**

Account Operation............................ 72

Market Order............................ 73

Limit Order 73

Stop Order............................ 75

Trailing Stop............................ 76

Stop Level............................ 77

Timing 79

Naked Put............................ 79

When to Sell and Move On............... **85**

Stopped Out 85

Buy-and-Hold............................ 86

Fundamental Changes 87
Shifting Values 88
Plan Your Investments **91**
Investing 91
Limit Your Exposure 92
Diversify 92
Use Stop Losses 92
Risk 93
Timing 93
Sources of Research **95**
About the Author **97**
Other Books **99**
Final Note **101**

Disclaimer and Risk Disclosure

By reading this book you agree that this book and any ideas expressed within are for informational and educational purposes only and do not constitute advice or recommendations. Trading in the stock market, whether for short or long-term purposes, is risky and may not be suitable for all investors. You must understand that you may lose any money invested.

Before you start share trading, you should carefully consider your financial situation, your level of experience and knowledge, and your appetite for risk. You could lose some or all of your trading capital, and you must understand how to mitigate that risk. No liability is accepted by Alan Northcott or his successors for any losses whether direct, indirect or consequential suffered by the use of any information contained herein.

The information given in this book is for educational and personal enjoyment purposes only, and is not a recommendation to enter into trading in any form. If any specific trading or investment or legal advice is required, the services of a competent and appropriately licensed person should be sought..

Introduction

The stock market – what image does that conjure in your mind? Do you think of screens of rapidly flashing numbers, traders in the pits waving wildly, as seen in many movies, or do you simply think of the stock market as a vehicle for financial growth?

Whatever your mental image, the chances are that it is or has been correct, for the stock market has many different faces. In this book I explain how you can take part in the stock market, and what to look for to try and make your involvement profitable.

People ask if you can really double your money in the stock market every seven years? Well, if you can choose which seven years in recent history you wan to look at, yes you can, and you can possibly do even better than that. The statistics say you should on average double your money, but the values change a lot from year to year, which means you cannot count on it for any particular period.

In this book, I touch on both investing and trading, but the emphasis is on long-term financial prospects, in other words investing. I have written and continue to write many books and articles about trading on the various markets available, and if you are interested in that aspect, I would be glad to recommend them to you.

Nevertheless, short-term trading is very different from investing for the longer-term, and while certain readers may have the time and the inclination for trading, it is a specialized subject and not suitable for everybody. On the other hand, investing is something that everyone should take part in, to grow his or her wealth.

I have set up a companion website to this book at **www.newbiesguidetostocks.com**. I hope you will visit it and look around, as I have reproduced all the diagrams there (for clarity) and have set up a forum for discussions and questions.

A.N.

What is a Stock?

Before we can go into discussing stock markets and what use they can be to you and your money, you need to understand what a stock is, and how it all works. This guide is for "newbies", so I am not assuming any previous knowledge on your part. If you already know about the stock market, simply skip the first three chapters or treat them as a refresher course.

Put simply, when you buy a stock you own a part of a company. This is because when the stock was originally created, usually with what is called the Initial Public Offering (IPO), the founders or owners of the company involved decided to sell part ownership in order to raise money for its operation.

You usually get some benefits or privileges from owning stocks, such as for instance sharing in the profits, but unless you are Warren Buffet or another major investor, you will probably not be recognized if you choose to visit the company.

That is because there are many shares issued, so you generally only own a very small part. For instance, Apple's shares are selling at several hundred dollars each, which may seem a reasonable amount to you, but you must consider that there are nearly 1,000,000,000 Apple shares on the market.

Incidentally, I used both the words stocks and shares above, and for our purposes, they are very similar. The difference is usually in the way the words used, with "stocks" commonly referring to shares in several different companies, and shares usually referring to holdings in one company only.

Although you only own a small part of the company, you may have a part to play in its running. There is always an Annual General Meeting or AGM that shareholders are invited to attend, and shareholders can influence a company's direction if they work together "en masse" on matters that are voted on there. In addition, shareholders often receive a regular income from the company.

Many years ago, shares were physical pieces of paper, and might be kept in a safety deposit box in a bank; nowadays, you will not receive any certificates, but simply have your shareholding recognized electronically. This change makes it easier when you want to buy and sell shares, which you can do online.

Some companies choose to remain privately owned for many years, which means they are owned by the founders, an investment group, or the people who work there and their friends, and shares are not offered to the general public. But if a company wants to raise a major amount of capital for research, expansion, or other purposes, then "going public" is a clearly defined path. It also allows the founders and original owners of the company to get back some of the money that they have invested.

There is a saying "Don't put all your eggs in one basket", and this applies to share ownership. You should not count on any one company, however great it seems, to grow your savings.

Market Sectors

Companies are classified into different fields of operation, such as mining, electronics, retail, etc., and you will usually aim to own a mix of these. This is for the simple reason that you do not want to be caught out if a single type of company or "market sector" as it is known suffers a downturn. You may remember more than 10 years ago when the "dot-com" companies were all the rage, then crashed when people realized that the value was not there. Anyone who was following just the high flyers, many of which were in the dot-com field, suddenly found themselves much poorer.

Company Size

In addition to having different market sectors, stocks can also be classified by the size of the company, with "large caps" being the largest multinational corporations, "mid-caps" the next but still very large companies, and "small caps". These classifications have standard definitions in terms of the total value of the company. The value of the company is calculated simply as the total number of shares issued multiplied by the share price. Not all companies are as large as even small caps, in fact many are not, though if you get down to the "micro" level of companies, they are likely to be more risky places to put your money.

Going Public

When a company issues shares to the public, it will do so with the "initial public offering" as mentioned above. At this stage, it has several choices. For instance, the original owners of the company can retain 50% or more of the value so that they have ultimate control and cannot have their company hijacked by new shareholders, or by a rival company seeking to buy them out. Alternatively, and depending on what the original owners want out of the issue, they can choose to sell off much of the value, and make more money for themselves.

In preparation for "going public", it is usual to employ financial advisers who take a look at the company and form an opinion of its overall value. They then recommend the value to be "floated" on the stock market. Even when the value has been decided, there is no rule on how many shares a company has to issue, for instance, the owners could choose to issue one million shares at $500 each, or 500 million shares at one dollar each, and that would amount to the same valuation.

Another factor for the valuation is that it always looks good if all the shares in the IPO are sold quickly, so the financial advisers try to anticipate the demand of the market when they set the price. Sometimes they will also try to guarantee that the shares will be sold by having private arrangements with pension funds and other major financial houses who will commit to buying a certain amount, and maybe even picking up shares that are not sold immediately.

You have probably heard tales of people making fortunes by simply buying IPOs and selling them a few weeks later after the price has risen 20% or more. That has happened, but it is not guaranteed. You simply have to look back at the recent Facebook IPO to realize that sometimes shares go down after they are first issued.

That said, the usual tendency is for share prices to go up soon after the initial public offering simply because the financial advisers try to set the price at an attractive level to ensure interest. As so many people have seen money being made with IPOs the demand has increased, allowing prices to be set higher. I will talk about supply and demand and its effect on prices in a later chapter.

Once the IPO has happened, the company has little to gain from the price of the shares. It got its money one time, with the IPO. When shares change hands later, that is purely between different investors. The people running the company may retain some shares so it is in their personal interest for the price to increase, but the company does not gain anything directly if the share price goes up.

What to Expect

However, the actions of the company can and do affect the share price. The share price has to anticipate future expectations of the value of the company, and is influenced by many factors such as how well the company is run, and how much profit is made. If the company pays a proportion of the profits in dividends, that too can affect the share price, and there will be more about valuing shares in a later chapter.

When the company declares a dividend or regular payment to shareholders, it is expressed as a certain amount per share. This means there is no requirement to hold a certain number of shares before you can receive a dividend. The amount you receive is calculated from the number of shares that you held on a particular date, around the time the dividend was announced. You do not have to hold them for any length of time, simply be the shareholder on that day. Shares traded after that date are called "ex-dividend" as the new shareholders will not receive the payout this time around.

How much the dividend is depends solely on the company. Many companies do not issue a dividend, preferring to reinvest any excess profit for growth. The total amount paid out any time a dividend is paid is usually a percentage of the profits, which allows some money to be plowed back into the company. Still, the dividend can be whatever the directors decide, and may even be more than the total profits if the directors decide to maintain a reliable dividend for shareholders. Though unusual, this could happen if there was a particularly bad quarter's trading, or a one-off loss hitting the books. Keeping the dividend constant or preferable slightly increasing keeps shareholders' confidence high, and the company stays well respected.

What happens when the price of shares that you own goes up and down? Nothing, immediately. You still own the same number of shares, and you can multiply that by the current price to see how much you could sell them for. It is only when you sell your shares that you actually make a profit or loss. Up until then it is purely a paper profit or loss.

Types of Holding

You may have heard the expressions "preferred stock" and "common stock". Common stock is what you normally buy, but sometimes a company will also issue preferred stock. With preferred stock you have extra privileges and rights, the chief of which may be that you're more likely to get some money back if the company goes bankrupt, though sometimes it includes different voting rights.

Companies can also issue bonds, on which they promise to pay interest. Basically these are a loan to the company, and as such are totally different from shares. As a bondholder, you should get your money back with interest per the bond contract. However, if the company goes broke, there is a pecking order for paying out what money remains and which can be raised from selling the company's property. The general creditors and bondholders are paid what is due to them first, then the preferred stockholders. Right at the end the common stockholders get what's left, if anything.

You should not allow the fact that you can lose all your money when you invest in common stock to bother you unduly. You would have to be extremely careless to let the situation get to that point before taking some action. It is all part of taking responsibility for your own investments, an important concept, and I will cover that later.

Stocks vs. Other Investments

You may have heard this fact before. Of all the places that you could have put your money for an investment, stocks are the ones that come out on top for returns, on average. In the last 50 years, the figures are about 8% per year average return on stocks, which goes up into double figures if you take into account dividend reinvestment, i.e. taking any dividends paid and reinvesting them in the stocks.

Stocks are also the only investment that has consistently beaten inflation over time; even bonds have given a negative return in some decades after accounting for inflation.

In a sense, that is what you should intuitively expect. When you put money in stocks, you are taking on more risk than buying bonds, so the returns should be greater. If not, that would be an unstable situation, and over the course of time, the relative values would have to change.

However, this fact about return on investment glosses over much of the detail. For instance, there have been many years when the value of your stock portfolio would be less at the end of the year than at the beginning, assuming you did not change anything. That is why you should only consider investing in the stock market for the long-term, when you can ride out the ups and downs. Trading, aimed at profiting from the ups and downs in the markets, requires a different set of abilities, and frequent dealing and attention to analysis.

If you are young enough to have a long-term horizon, then the statistics show that you should make more profit over the years from investing in stocks than any other buy-and-hold investment; but you may have to tolerate some swings in value. Other analysis shows that if you were out of the market on as little as 50 critical days in recent decades, then your returns would be decimated, so unless you're prepared to risk missing out, you need to hang in there and stay fully committed.

Mutual Funds

Where else might you be tempted to put your funds for the long-term? A mutual fund is one of the obvious answers. A mutual fund has the supposed great advantage that it is a fund for investors and it is actively managed by experts, who put the pool of money where they think it will do best.

Of course, the mutual fund managers and support staff need paying, so the fund will levy a small annual charge, say 1% or 2%. A small price for access to all that expertise, you may think.

If you think that, you probably have not heard the statistic that the majority of mutual funds do worse than the overall market that they are investing in. Whether it is emerging markets, technologies companies, or the overall stock market, many funds do not serve you well. You might do better to put your money in a basically unmanaged fund that simply tracks the value of the overall market by investing in a fixed range of shares.

Note that mutual funds may have front-end and/or backend loads or charges, and while this is usually quite clear if you know to watch out for them, they can also have 12b-1 fees which are additional commissions paid annually to the broker. If you decide to buy funds rather than individual stocks, then at least you should know that it is not necessary to buy a fund that has additional fees attached, as with good selection you can find "no load" funds that perform as well. Even then, by their nature of mutual funds have annual charges to cover management and administrative fees so you must select the best value.

I do not wish to single out mutual funds vendors, as all types of financial products can be loaded with transaction fees and commissions. You can find out more about mutual funds from my Mutual Fund book, which will guide you if you want to make this type of investment.

Other Funds

If instead you choose an index fund, which by definition should require less in management fees, you still want to be sure that you get it from a large discount company such as Schwab or Fidelity. While your broker is required by the Securities and Exchange Commission to tell you the fees he charges if you ask, the chances are that he has no clear idea, and would have to dig out the paperwork, check on the trading commissions, loads, and wrap fees before he could answer it.

Managed Accounts

Managed accounts include mutual funds, but also any other account where you hand control of your money over to someone else for them to decide what investments to make. Some of these arrangements work out well, and some not so well, as it comes down to the experience, knowledge and commitment of the manager, as well as to the way the markets are working.

In some financial circles, you will hear the term "alpha" banded about. Alpha is regarded as a good thing, and the higher the better. Alpha is a measure of how a managed investment did against the market as a whole, and is commonly used when referring to mutual fund managers and the like. If the manager has a high alpha, then he does quite well for his clients, "beating the market" consistently.

The market as a whole in this case is usually well defined, and will be an index of all or selected shares, whatever the fund is investing in. The index may be the value of all shares in a market, added together in proportion to their value, or something more refined such as the Dow Jones Industrial Average (shortened to the "Dow") which is calculated from the value of 30 shares selected by the publishers of the Wall Street Journal.

Does alpha exist, and how do you find it? In other words, can some people consistently beat the market? At best, only a few. The answer should not surprise you, if you read the previous section about mutual funds. About 75% of the managed funds you can buy do not keep up with the market index. This is in part because managed funds need to make a charge for their services, to pay for the manager and administration, but it is still a disappointing reality about using managed funds for your investments.

Savings Accounts

I guess if you have looked at the interest rates available on savings accounts recently, you have probably already dismissed this option for yourself. The interest is not enough to cover inflation, let alone grow your funds.

Property Investment

Another alternative is to become a landlord, buying properties and renting them out. Until the property bubble burst, this looked like a no-lose proposition, with every one of your rental properties increasing steadily in value while your tenants' rents provided reasonable returns on your capital, or paid your mortgage if you had borrowed the money.

I would advocate considering property investment as a part of your portfolio, but you need to weigh up carefully the possible problems and downsides. If you manage the properties yourself, you must be on call 24 hours a day to fix or arrange repair for problems such as leaking water heaters. If instead you employ a rental agent, they will typically take about 10% of the rent, and that may be enough to turn a positive cash flow into a negative cash flow.

Crowd Funding

Crowd funding is a recent addition to places to put your money. It allows you to invest in businesses and people who put their ideas out there to attract investors. The laws have been changed to allow anyone to invest any amount in a business – previously, you might have to be "an accredited investor" which means you have an income of $200,000 a year or a net worth of more than $1 million. This was a restriction based on the idea that only wealthy people should take part in risky investments. The same restriction is placed on anyone wanting to invest in a hedge fund.

This sort of spending, putting money in startup or microcap companies, is not for the inexperienced. It has potential, but you have to be aware of the risks, and be prepared for big swings in your fortune.

Summary

One final point about why you might decide to invest in stocks as opposed to other places. It allows you to put your money in something that interests you, and that can be exciting to keep an eye on. Some people choose to make their own personal statements by where they invest, say for instance putting money in green technology companies in preference to industrial polluters. Whatever your motivations, stock investing can certainly interest you more than locking your money away in a bank.

As you will read later, even if you have a long time horizon I do not advocate putting all your savings in the stock market, but you should spread the risk around. After reading this book, you may still decide to use a financial advisor to guide you on your investments, but it is my hope that you will bring your newfound knowledge to bear, and make sure that you question and understand their advice.

The type of advisor or broker that you use is very important for your financial health. You do not want an advisor who is paid any sort of commission for selling you products, and you are entitled to ask about this when you first meet.

In addition, you should watch out for advisors who only offer one type of financial product. This may make them experts on the particular product, such as mutual funds, but if mutual funds are not the best answer for you, they are not likely to suggest the alternatives that they are not familiar with.

How the Stock Market Works

Having decided that the stocks are at least worth a look for some investment, the next step is to see how they are bought and sold, and talk about how the stock market works.

You know that a market, such as the eBay marketplace, is a place where things are bought and sold. So it is with a stock market, with millions of stocks changing hands each day. There are many different stock markets in the world, with most developed countries having at least one, and the United States having several, such as the New York Stock Exchange, the NASDAQ, the National Stock Exchange, several exchanges in Chicago including also options and futures trading . . . and the list goes on.

Some exchanges specialize in particular types of markets or stocks. Some stocks, particularly of larger companies, are offered on several different exchanges, with the prices kept in sync by modern technology to avoid "arbitrage", which is where computers or quick dealers used to be able to take advantage of differences in prices to make guaranteed profits.

Stock dealings

All dealings in major public shares go through a stock exchange, but you cannot go to a stock exchange and buy and sell shares. You have to use an authorized dealer or stockbroker. They in turn connect with the people on the floor of the stock exchange, the traders, who are responsible for making and keeping an active market in the shares.

The mechanics of this doesn't really matter to you, as in practice you will simply deal with a broker who takes care of buying and selling shares on your behalf. The process is virtually instantaneous, most of the time. There is more about types of broker in a later chapter.

So if you decided you wanted to buy 100 shares in a company, you could instruct your broker and he would get you 100 shares at the price then current. Sometimes the broker will keep his own reserve of shares in hand, so your small order of 100 shares may not even get to the trading floor but be taken out of his reserve – but that is for him to decide as part of his operating procedure.

Some people are puzzled how you can buy more shares when all the authorized shares were already sold at the IPO. The answer is that the traders have to find a shareholder who is willing to sell at a certain price. The number of shares in circulation does not change. This is all part of the way that shares change in value, and go up and down in price because of supply and demand, and that is discussed later.

Stock Splits

There is an exception to this rule, and that is when the company decides to do a stock split. The company may for instance say that for every old share it will give you 10 new shares. This sort of thing is usually done when the price of the original shares has increased so much that it is a disincentive to trading in the stock. It does not in itself change the overall value of the company, though it may stimulate more interest and demand.

An example of this was when Berkshire Hathaway, the company run by Warren Buffett, decided in 2010 to split each of its Class B shares then trading at $3400 into 50 new shares, which would then be about $68 each. This allowed access to people with less to invest. They became relatively affordable, particularly when you realize that Berkshire Hathaway's premium shares, the Class A, cost well over $100,000 each (only the Class A shares have voting rights).

Occasionally you will have a company do a "reverse stock split", which is the opposite thing, reducing the number of shares held by existing stockholders while raising the value of the new shares – again, in itself not a change in the overall valuation of the company.

This particular action is generally considered very negative, and is usually taken by a company that is not doing well. It can be required if a company wants to stay listed on a certain stock exchange, where there is a minimum value for shares. For example, the NASDAQ may delist shares that fall below one dollar.

Delisting

As a side note, companies that get delisted, that is, taken off the books at the stock market, can continue to have their stocks traded on the "pink sheets", the so-called over-the-counter market. This consists of brokers or dealers trading with each other directly. It's not considered good for the average investor to consider OTC stocks, as companies there may be delisted for infringements, have bad credit records, or are otherwise unable to make the listing requirements of the Securities and Exchange Commission (SEC), the financial regulating body which protects your interests. As there is less trading in general, you can find that the dealing is "illiquid", which means it is hard to find someone to take the other side of your order, and consequently prices can swing wildly.

Share Options

Sometimes you will be able to buy some shares, usually in the company where you work, by exercising share options. These may be given as an incentive or a bonus to staff, and allow the recipients to buy shares at a certain bargain price. Once again, they don't create new shares but would simply come out of the shares that the company retained ownership of, and did not sell initially on the market, or shares it has bought back.

Share options as described should not be confused with options on shares. Option trading is a completely different financial exercise, and if you're interested in finding out about that there are many good books, including the bestselling one for newbies in this series, which is referenced at the beginning and end of this book.

Takeovers

When one company takes over another company, this means that the first company buys a controlling interest in the second company, in simple terms more than 50% of the shares. Although in theory it could just go and buy the shares on the open market, there are various reasons that this does not happen, and usually existing shareholders are able to decide on an offer made to them as a whole.

The problem with a company simply buying 50% of the shares through the stock exchange is that it cannot do this stealthily. There are statutory regulations that require this to be done openly, and that would change the dynamics on how the remaining shareholders felt about selling.

So what happens to the value of the shares, when there is a takeover attempt? Well, they will certainly fluctuate, but what happens depends on the market's mood towards the offer and the ongoing prospects of the combined operation. Often the company taking over will set a higher price than the current list price for shares of the other company, giving an incentive for existing shareholders to agree and sell them the required number of stocks. Sometimes there will be a deal where stocks are exchanged, each stockholder in the company receiving a certain number of shares in the one taking over, in recompense.

Then again, takeovers can also fail if the offer does not seem attractive enough, and not enough existing shareholders decide to sell up. It can be an exciting time financially, and you need to know what you are doing and have some insight into the company's operations to be sure of coming out ahead.

Bankruptcy

If a company ceases trading and files for bankruptcy, that is another unpredictable situation. As mentioned previously, the ordinary shareholders get what is left after everyone else is paid out, so they are not likely to get their money back with a company that is running out of funds.

Occasionally, after a moment of silence at the end of an old friend, unscrupulous directors of the old company may decide to start up a new fresh company, clear of all debts and credit defaults. The new company would have no liability for the old company's debts, unless any of the directors had specifically assumed personal liability. This sort of situation is usually monitored and is regulated by the authorities to avoid what may be seen as a name change of convenience.

Why a Stock Price Changes

Now we come to what is really the point of the discussion. What affects the stock price, and by implication how can we anticipate price changes so that we can profit from them?

There are almost as many answers to this question as there are expert stock pickers. Very few financial advisers can consistently make money, which is why they sell newsletters and gain commissions from investing for others. Once you understand the ideas behind stock price movement, you will be nearly as well equipped to answer this question as they are.

Supply and Demand

If you remember any economics, you should know about supply and demand. Supply and demand through the mechanism of the market sets the price of anything. When supply goes up or demand comes down, then you can expect the price to fall; if the supply drops or the demand goes up, that puts pressure on the price to increase.

If there are thousands of blue widgets, the price may fall. It may even become impossible to give them away. But supposing there is any demand at all for blue widgets, if there are only a few available you can charge a lot for them.

In the same way, suppose demand for blue widgets goes up because they have been featured on a television show, or some popular celebrity recommends them. Without an increasing supply, the price is bound to rise. On the other hand, when demand falls away, say because the color is shown to rub off and stain your hands, then the price will drop.

The fundamental forces of supply and demand are always working in every market. In fact, the price is often lagging behind so it is only over time that it catches up and strikes a balance between the two forces. As stockbrokers buy and sell stocks, the supply and demand are constantly changing, causing the continual fluctuations in price.

If the price goes up and down a lot, then the stock is said to have a high volatility. If the price is fairly constant, then it is exhibiting a low volatility. Volatility is relative, and is often compared to similar stocks in the same market to see if the particular volatility should be considered high or low.

Making Money

When you invest in stocks, you may expect to make money in two distinct ways. First, you hope to pick stocks whose price may go up over time. This may be because the current price of the stock is less than it really deserves, and sooner or later the market comes to its senses and realizes the true value; or it may be because the company is in a booming industry, and you expect the company to sell more products year after year, growing its operation. Sometimes these two reasons for an increase in stock price are identified as "investing for value" or "investing for growth".

The second way that you hope to make money is by receiving dividends from the company, usually paid out quarterly when they are offered. Dividends are not paid out on all shares, as it depends on the corporate policy. With dividend paying shares, companies will usually try to increase the returns slightly each year, satisfying the shareholders that the company is healthy.

You are looking at two discrete ways of making money. If the share price grows, then you have capital gain on paper, but no more money until you choose to sell some shares. If you receive dividends, then you get a regular income without affecting your shareholding. If you do not happen to need the income, it is a good idea to allow the dividends to reinvest in the shares, compounding your gains, and there are automatic ways to do this.

Estimating Worth

When you have a dividend-paying share, you have a relatively easy way to derive a reasonable price for the share. You simply look at how much you get in dividends as a return on your capital, and compare that with interest paid from putting money elsewhere, for example in bonds or a savings account. Put in your own factor for how safe or risky you think the stocks are, and you can derive a reasonable value. This may not be the most accurate result, but it gives you a calculated starting point.

On the other hand, with shares that have no dividends, the price is a reflection of future value expectations, and much more troublesome to analyze. Simplistically, the very least that shares should be worth is the money that could be made from a distressed sale of all company's equipment and real estate if the company ceased operation, but in real life a viable company has a much greater value than that, including the value of its reputation, copyrights, and goodwill.

When you are considering what the future value of the shares may be, you should take account of the discounted value of money in the future. For example, due to inflation $100 ten years from now is not the same as $100 in your hand right now. The economists have various formulas to work this out, and you can do that too. But at the end of the day, you are probably going to simply compare investing in one company to investing in another, so you are just looking for the better choice rather than the theoretical absolute value.

Does Analysis Work?

I mentioned previously that many managers of funds seem to do less well than the market as whole, despite it being their job to stay on top of trends and pick the winners. This might lead you to think that there is no way to select stocks, and little point in trying to do so.

That was the way some people thought about 50 years ago, and it provided a great boost for a theory called the Efficient Market Hypothesis (EMH). This states that it is impossible to consistently beat the market as the stock price always reflects all available information. The conclusion is that it is effectively pointless trying to analyze stocks to find an edge.

This in turn was the development of a previous theory developed in the 19th century, the Random Walk Theory, which asserted that stock price fluctuations were basically random.

Certainly, there is an argument for the EMH. Simply put, if a price of the stock is cheaper than it should be according to all the information available to investors, then those investors would seek to profit by buying the stock. This in turn would increase the demand and push the price up. Similarly, if the price is too high according to available information, then the shareholders would sell to capture the profit before the price came down to the right value, and this increase in supply would lower the price. Therefore in either case the price would tend towards a "true" value, whatever that may be.

Notice that the Efficient Market Hypothesis does not say the price is always correct, simply that you and anyone else cannot know if it is too high or too low. Believers therefore say that it is pointless to search for undervalued stocks, or even to try and predict trends.

This theory has been argued about for years, and some people will still maintain it is correct. However, you have only to look at history to identify how some people are able to consistently succeed, most notably Warren Buffett who has over and over again beaten the market over many decades.

Similarly, some technical traders make a good living out of short term trading. If the Efficient Market Hypothesis was correct in practice, this would not be possible.

You might argue that stock analysis is self-fulfilling, in that if analysis says the price is going up, investors will buy the stock and therefore make the price go up. So what? Why it works does not really matter as long as we can be reasonably confident that analysis does work, and is therefore a worthwhile exercise.

Types of Analysis

There are two distinct ways that stocks are analyzed, and while you should be familiar with both of them, you will probably concentrate on one method, depending what you want out of your stock investment.

If you are interested in buying stocks that will grow in value over the years, perhaps paying increasing dividends, then you want to know that you have invested in a sound and well-managed company with good prospects for the future. The usual way to gauge this, which I will go into in detail in the next chapter, is to use "fundamental analysis".

The other method, which is familiar to stock traders, is called "technical analysis". This is geared toward short-term fluctuations, and is used by short-term traders who may buy and sell stocks on an hourly, daily, or weekly basis. It concentrates much more on the emotion and sentiment of market traders, which is the driving force behind the supply and demand that creates continual price fluctuations.

While everyone should have some solid long-term financial investments, whether stocks or other financial instruments, short-term trading is discretionary and requires a different approach, both mentally and in analysis.

In the future I will be producing a newbies' guide to technical analysis in this book series, and if you are interested drop me a line at AlanNorthcott@msn.com and I will let you know when it's done. A knowledge of technical analysis can be useful even for the long-term investor, as it will allow you to pick a good time to make your investment, and hopefully avoid any immediate losses.

To repeat, the value or price of a stock depends on the market's perception of it, and anticipation of its future performance. Variations in the way that a company and its stock is regarded can make short-term fluctuations which a trader can exploit for profit. In the long-term, it is the basic foundations of the company and its operation which will impact the price.

The long-term investor is quite prepared to keep hold of shares in a good company, despite minor fluctuations; the short-term trader looks for the fluctuations from which to profit. Two different approaches with a similar goal, but different timing and expectations.

Doing The Numbers

Building on what you now know about how stock prices change, we will look at the factors which are important when you are selecting a stock for investment. This is for a stock that you expect to hold on to for some time, and while stellar growth would be great, we are really looking for steady above average growth in value.

Fundamental analysis requires looking at balance sheets, examining growth or decline in the relevant markets as well as the company, and many other common sense factors. Much of the information you need to find out is available online, either at the company's website or at a more general financial website, and considering that you expect to hold the shares for some time, it is well worth taking a little time to do your research.

The goal of your research is to identify stocks that appear to be undervalued, that may possibly be already increasing in price, and that represent a relatively safe harbor for your funds. Here are some of the methods and numbers used.

P/E Ratio

To determine if shares are undervalued, you need to have a means of assessing what their true value is. I have already mentioned that we can form some judgments about a company from dividends, if the company issues dividends.

Dividends usually come out of the company's earnings, so one of the first places many people look is the published earnings of a company. This leads to our first value ratio, the price/earnings or P/E ratio. Here you compare the stock price with the company's earnings. As mentioned previously, dividends paid out are not directly related to the company's earnings, but over time dividends can only come out from the earnings, so the earnings are important.

You will find tables of these figures for every company in the financial pages of the newspapers, or online. The P/E ratio is the share price in dollars divided by the earnings per share in dollars. The P/E ratio averages around 15 for all companies in the market, and different market sectors tend to have slightly different average P/E ratios.

What can you learn from the P/E ratio? One thing you can do is work out the current earnings yield of the shares. This is simply the earnings divided by the stock value, multiplied by 100%. For a P/E ratio of 15, this would be 1/15 x 100, which is 6.7%. Given that a P/E of 15 is typical, from this simple calculation you can see why stocks in general are favored over bonds and savings accounts for providing good returns in the long run.

At this time, I must point out one potential problem with the P/E ratio. There are different ways to calculate it, and commonly you will see the current stock price compared to the previous 12 months' earnings. Sometimes the numbers are based on projected future earnings, and sometimes half-and-half, past and future. You can probably see there might be a problem with figures differing, depending on the method used.

Now as this is not a perfect world, we often have to deal with the best information that we have. You simply need to be aware that things are not as cut and dried as you may wish. If you are doing any comparisons between companies, try to make sure that they are at least using the same standard.

Although the P/E ratio is widely used by investors as a primary qualification for further research, you should note that the well-known investor, William J O'Neil, who founded the Investors Business Daily, said that the P/E ratio was less important to him than the company's actual earnings, and the rate of increase in the earnings year on year.

P/S Ratio

The other potential problem with the P/E ratio is that earnings figures can be manipulated by the company's accountants, perhaps changing or bringing forward expenses to set against earnings, according to the desires of the management. This means that some investors prefer to use the P/S ratio, the price/sales ratio instead.

Because the sales figures do not take into account any expenses or debt, they are less able to be manipulated to give an embellished statement of the company's financial position.

P/B Ratio

A third ratio that is of interest to investors is the P/B ratio, the price/book ratio. This compares the share price to the "book price" of the firm, which is what the accountants figure out it is worth. Once again, you are in the hands of the accountants to some extent, looking at the figures that they generate. However, there are standard procedures to work out a company's book value, so this cannot be manipulated too much.

In general terms, when working out the book value the accountants usually take the company's asset value as a starting point, and subtract the company's debts and liabilities. A low P/B ratio will quite often mean that the company is undervalued, unless there are any other reasons for it. On the other hand, a high P/B ratio, say over 2, probably means that the stocks are overpriced.

Debt Ratio

As part of your research, you need to look at how much debt a company tends to run on. Companies usually have to take on debt when they are starting up or undergoing major expansion. With some that have been established for some time, much of the debt may have been paid back.

Debt in itself is not necessarily a problem, and some types of company tend to run more debt than others. However, the debt has to be serviced, at least paying interest for borrowing the money, and the payments come out of any potential profits. With a high level of debt, the company is much more vulnerable to changes in interest rates, and this can cause a problem beyond the company's immediate control.

The amount of debt is usually quoted in the form of the Debt Ratio, which is simply the ratio of the amount of debt compared to the total share value of the company. A typical Debt Ratio may be around 25%, and anything over 60% may be a problem, for the reasons mentioned above. As with all the other ratios, one way to check whether the ratio might be considered excessive is to compare it to the equivalent ratios of other companies in the same line of business.

Sources of Information

Now that you have an idea of some of the numbers, it is time to introduce you to where you can find them. Most company websites will give you access to the "financials", but it is easier if you go to a financial website such as **finance.yahoo.com** which will allow you to access many different companies' statistics.

The layout of the page changes from time to time, but at the moment the web address given above will open to the latest financial news. There is a search box at the top, and you can enter the name or ticker symbol of the company. If you choose name, a drop-down will give you choices between the different financial instruments, and you have to select the correct ticker symbol.

Going with IBM as an example again, and choosing the NYSE (New York Stock Exchange) in preference to the quotes from other countries, takes you to a financial summary page that also contains the latest news. This is the summary for today: –

This gives the P/E, earnings, beta, and dividend numbers as a starting point for your research.

Lower down on the left side, under the heading Financials, you will find Income Statement, Balance Sheet, and Cash Flow. This gives you more detailed information, and while it is a lot to digest there are some gems to be had.

For instance, if you suspect that a company is manipulating its earnings you can check it out here.

On the Cash Flow screen, check out the cash flow from operating activities, as in the example below.

View: **Annual Data** | Quarterly Data   All numbers in thousands

Period Ending	Dec 31, 2012	Dec 31, 2011	Dec 31, 2010
Net Income	16,604,000	15,855,000	14,833,000
Operating Activities, Cash Flows Provided By or Used In			
Depreciation	4,676,000	4,815,000	4,831,000
Adjustments To Net Income	756,000	1,567,000	1,122,000
Changes In Accounts Receivables	(2,230,000)	(1,279,000)	(489,000)
Changes In Liabilities	(1,232,000)	(920,000)	(1,789,000)
Changes In Inventories	280,000	(163,000)	92,000
Changes In Other Operating Activities	730,000	(28,000)	949,000
Total Cash Flow From Operating Activities	19,586,000	19,846,000	19,549,000
Investing Activities, Cash Flows Provided By or Used In			
Capital Expenditures	(4,082,000)	(4,108,000)	(4,185,000)
Investments	(1,575,000)	1,460,000	1,343,000
Other Cash flows from Investing Activities	(3,348,000)	(1,748,000)	(5,666,000)
Total Cash Flows From Investing Activities	(9,004,000)	(4,396,000)	(8,507,000)
Financing Activities, Cash Flows Provided By or Used In			
Dividends Paid	(3,773,000)	(3,473,000)	(3,177,000)
Sale Purchase of Stock	(10,455,000)	(12,593,000)	(11,601,000)
Net Borrowings	2,252,000	2,370,000	2,350,000
Other Cash Flows from Financing Activities	-	-	-
Total Cash Flows From Financing Activities	(11,976,000)	(13,696,000)	(12,429,000)
Effect Of Exchange Rate Changes	(116,000)	(493,000)	(135,000)
Change In Cash and Cash Equivalents	(1,511,000)	1,262,000	(1,522,000)

IBM is reporting $19,586,000,000 (all numbers are in thousands, as noted in the top right). If this number was low or negative then you would know that the company did not bring in any real money with its business in the previous year.

Next check out the Income Statement and look for the net income. In IBM's case this turns out to be $16,604,000,000, see below.

View: **Annual Data**	Quarterly Data			All numbers in thousands
Period Ending	Dec 31, 2012	Dec 31, 2011	Dec 31, 2010
Total Revenue	104,507,000	106,916,000	99,870,000
Cost of Revenue	54,209,000	56,778,000	53,857,000
Gross Profit	50,298,000	50,138,000	46,014,000
Operating Expenses			
Research Development	6,302,000	6,258,000	6,026,000
Selling General and Administrative	22,479,000	22,486,000	20,683,000
Non Recurring	-	-	-
Others	-	-	-
Total Operating Expenses	-	-	-
Operating Income or Loss	21,517,000	21,394,000	19,305,000
Income from Continuing Operations			
Total Other Income/Expenses Net	843,000	20,000	787,000
Earnings Before Interest And Taxes	22,361,000	21,414,000	20,091,000
Interest Expense	459,000	411,000	368,000
Income Before Tax	21,902,000	21,003,000	19,723,000
Income Tax Expense	5,298,000	5,148,000	4,890,000
Minority Interest	-	-	-
Net Income From Continuing Ops	16,604,000	15,855,000	14,833,000
Non-recurring Events			
Discontinued Operations	-	-	-
Extraordinary Items	-	-	-
Effect Of Accounting Changes	-	-	-
Other Items	-	-	-
Net Income	16,604,000	15,855,000	14,833,000
Preferred Stock And Other Adjustments	-	-	-
Net Income Applicable To Common Shares	16,604,000	15,855,000	14,833,000

This is healthy, as you might expect with IBM. If you found the company was reporting a decent income, but did not have much cash flow on the previous page, that would be a big red flag.

On the balance sheet tab you can check into the company's total assets. In IBM's case, these amount to $119,213,000,000, as shown on the extract from the balance sheet page below.

View: **Annual Data** | Quarterly Data   All numbers in thousands

Period Ending	Dec 31, 2012	Dec 31, 2011	Dec 31, 2010
Assets			
Current Assets			
Cash And Cash Equivalents	10,412,000	11,922,000	10,661,000
Short Term Investments	717,000	-	990,000
Net Receivables	31,993,000	31,162,000	29,789,000
Inventory	2,287,000	2,595,000	2,450,000
Other Current Assets	4,024,000	5,249,000	4,226,000
Total Current Assets	49,433,000	50,928,000	48,116,000
Long Term Investments	17,833,000	15,671,000	16,326,000
Property Plant and Equipment	13,996,000	13,883,000	14,096,000
Goodwill	29,247,000	26,213,000	25,136,000
Intangible Assets	3,787,000	3,392,000	3,488,000
Accumulated Amortization	-	-	-
Other Assets	945,000	2,843,000	3,068,000
Deferred Long Term Asset Charges	3,973,000	3,503,000	3,220,000
Total Assets	119,213,000	116,433,000	113,452,000
Liabilities			
Current Liabilities			
Accounts Payable	22,492,000	21,464,000	22,204,000
Short/Current Long Term Debt	9,181,000	8,463,000	6,778,000
Other Current Liabilities	11,952,000	12,197,000	11,580,000
Total Current Liabilities	43,625,000	42,123,000	40,562,000
Long Term Debt	24,088,000	22,857,000	21,846,000
Other Liabilities	28,025,000	27,370,000	24,204,000
Deferred Long Term Liability Charges	4,491,000	3,847,000	3,666,000
Minority Interest	124,000	97,000	126,000
Negative Goodwill	-	-	-

If you take the net income away from the cash flow, you get $2,982,000,000, and dividing by the total assets you finish up with 2 1/2%. This is totally reasonable. You should watch out if the percentage is more than plus or minus 10% as this would suggest earnings manipulations.

There are many other things you can discover about a company by delving through these financial tables. Another exercise that you may undertake is comparing different companies in the same market sector that you are considering, and see which are better or worse than each other.

Yahoo is one of the financial websites available to you, and there are several others. You should be careful to be sure that whatever site you use is an independent one with no ties to any of the companies being rated, and then your comparisons will be valid. Incidentally, if the diagrams in this are too small to read easily, then that you can find them repeated on the companion website to this book, **www.newbiesguidetostocks.com**.

You may have noticed a "beta" mentioned on the IBM summary page, with a value of 0.76. This is significant in financial circles. Beta is a measure of the volatility or fluctuation in price of a stock compared to the general market. A beta of 1.0 means that the stock price varies in a similar way to the overall market, a beta of 2.0 means that the price varies twice as much as the market, whether going up or down, and a beta of 0.0 means that market fluctuations don't seem to have any effect on the stock price. You can even have a negative beta, so a beta of minus 1.0 means that the stock price goes down as much as the market is going up, and vice versa.

Beta is worked out for you and available at many financial sites. It is not a constant, but should tend to remain about the same given similar operating conditions. It is a measure of how much risk or excitement you are in for when you choose a particular stock.

Looking at Charts

The technical trader is likely to look at charts a great deal. This is because technical analysis and short-term trading depend on the sentiment of the market and other traders' whims, and these are most clearly determined by technical indicators which are calculated from the historic values shown on the chart.

As an investor, you should adopt a different attitude towards price charts. You are not looking for minor fluctuations to make a quick profit, but most usually looking for major trends that you can invest in and ride as they go up. This can be one of your selection criteria when you come to pick your investments. You still need to do your fundamental analysis to determine that the company is sound enough to satisfy whatever investment rules you have adopted.

The idea of investing in a stock which is already going up comes from what is called the Dow Theory, which in its simplest form suggests that a trend once underway is likely to continue for a considerable time, subject to minor corrections in price which run contrary to the trend.

When the minor corrections become long enough and significant enough that they are greater than the previous ones, then the theory states that the main trend may be finishing, and perhaps even reversing, meaning the investment should be closed.

The Dow Theory covers several other points, but they are more applicable to short-term trading so will not be discussed here. The key to being able to apply this idea of investing in a stock which is already going up is to be able to identify a solid trend, and be fairly sure that it is not just a "blip".

One way that investors can see if a stock is improving in price is by plotting moving averages on the chart. These are a standard indicator available with any charting software, and all you have to do is decide how many days or periods you want them to average. The more periods you use, the smoother the moving average line, and the more disconnected it is from day-to-day fluctuations.

Typically a short-term trader would look at perhaps 5 or 10 day moving averages, maybe in conjunction with a 20 day average; for a longer view, the moving average may be calculated from as much as 200 days to identify a long-term move.

What Is A Trend?

Most people think they can simply look at the chart and spot whether there is a trend. To some extent, this is true, but the trend depends on what scale of chart you are looking at. For example, look at this chart of IBM, which comes from the MSN investing site **http://money.msn.com/stocks/**: –

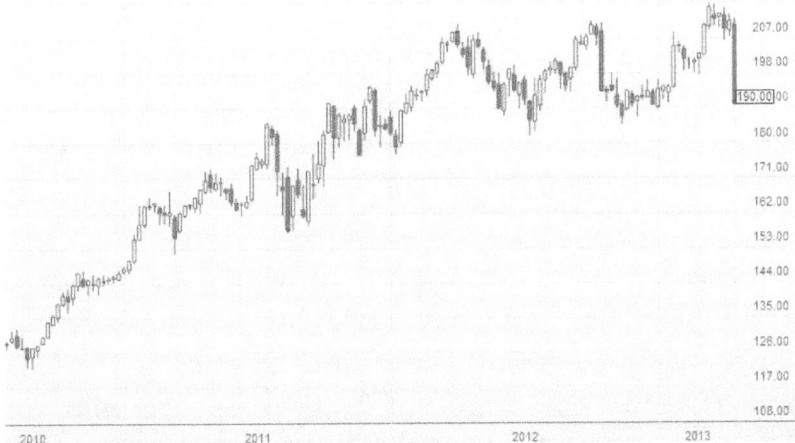

This covers the years 2010 to 2013, and most people would say there is a clear uptrend here. If pressed, you might say that the uptrend goes from the left until the middle, and after that it's a bit iffy, and though generally climbing you probably wouldn't want to have had your money invested in it after the midpoint.

Analysts like to define things, and one of the common analyst definitions of an uptrend is that the price makes successively higher low points, in other words each time the price dips down it doesn't go as far until it comes back up again. That means you can draw a line connecting the low points, and this will slope up (for an uptrend). This is called a "trendline".

Although we're not generally talking about "going short" on a stock, which is the trading practice of seeking to profit from a fall in price, when considering investing for the long-term, you should note that you can also have downward sloping trend lines when the price is consistently falling. These are drawn by connecting the successively lower high points of the price.

The problem which most analysts don't directly address when they explain how to draw a trendline is that there are many different ways to interpret the information, even with such a clear-cut definition. You can start drawing an upward trendline when you have two low point reversals simply by connecting them and extending the line onwards, but this may not be the best trendline or the one you finish up with. The timescale can make a great difference to how the trend appears.

Here is the same IBM graph with a few trend lines drawn on it: –

Each of these trend lines can be considered valid by the definition given, but you can see the different results.

There is one long trendline stretching across the graph, which would suggest that the uptrend continued across the period, though the red line stock price on the right-hand side has now dropped below it which usually is taken as a change of trend. This trendline represents a long-term view.

If you look at each of the shorter lines, they connect low points that are a month or more apart, and show different slopes. If you had followed each of these instead, and sold your investment when the price went below it, you would have made much more money than simply buying and holding the shares for the whole duration. But do you want to be trading every few months with your long-term funds?

There is no right or wrong answer to what to do; I am pointing it out so that you will give it some thought instead of blindly following the guidelines. If you look at charts on too short a timescale, then you will be buying and selling a lot more, effectively short-term trading; if your timescale is too long, then you might find that you are riding the price down too often, reducing some of your potential gains.

Unless you are prepared to check on your investments frequently, drawing trend lines as necessary, then you may find it better to stick with the longer timescale and accept some reduction in the amount of your gains. You need to consider what you will be happy with.

What Strategies Can You Use?

The strategies that you use will be fundamental to how your portfolio of stocks and shares performs. Unlike the trading market, where you may receive "hot tips" from various so-called advisors, with long-term investing you have time to research the companies yourself and make sure that they comply with whatever rules you decide are important for the security of your money.

Unlike some pundits, I do not recommend one particular method and eschew any others. I believe it is up to you, your personal financial position, your temperament and your propensity for risk what position you take in the markets. I can point out what has worked for others in the past, though that is no guarantee of future results. But I do think you need to be informed so that you can make your own choices.

There are investment newsletters, and some are fairly consistent in giving good advice. Many are not, and seem to exist either to flatter the egos of the writers or to pad the wallets of the publishers. After all, if the advice was consistently so good, why even bother with the trouble of assembling a team of writers, editors, and layout specialists? Why wouldn't you simply make great choices after great choices, and live richly beyond measure? In any case, you need to form your own opinion on any investment that you are considering.

Simplest First

To get the ball rolling, consider first a strategy for picking good stocks that is extremely simple. With the idea that you expect company performance to be reasonably consistent over time, you simply invest your money in the companies which have performed the best recently.

This depends on the seemingly logical concept that good management and sound markets can be reasonably relied upon, in other words that the star performer last year is not going to be the worst performer this and vice versa.

Therefore you can set aside a date each year when you review your portfolio. Consistent with your ideas about diversification of markets, you look at the previous year's performance of all stocks and pick the ones that made the most.

With just a brief check to make sure there are no extraordinary circumstances, i.e. ones which would not repeat this year, which caused the best performances; and perhaps another check to see that there are no looming problems for the coming year; you can go ahead and buy the bunch of stocks that you have identified. If you are already invested, this may involve selling some of your holdings, though obviously if the same company comes up again you can just hang onto the shares that you already have.

That's it, all done until next year. I advise keeping an eye on your investments while not fretting over their inevitable ups and downs – just in case something terrible happens. But you probably shouldn't need to take any action on your portfolio.

As a side note, you may want to leave your investments for a year and a day as a minimum. Under current tax laws, you will find that long-term capital gains, that is gains on shares you have held for more than a year, are treated differently from short-term or trading gains. It will generally work out in your favor to have your gains considered as long-term gains.

Momentum

I have already touched on momentum in the previous chapter. In its simplest expression, it simply says that a stock that is going up (or down) will carry on in that direction for a while unless something happens to change the circumstances. The momentum investor simply has to find the stocks which exhibit the best momentum, however that may be defined, invest and watch as the prices continue to rise.

From a practical point of view you might choose to look at the moving averages to see when an uptrend is established. In this case you will see that a shorter-term moving average rises up through a longer term moving average when the stock is starting a strong uptrend.

What about Dividends?

You will find many advisers who see dividends as the key to stock selection. You can calculate the dividend yield of a stock by dividing the annual dividend payment in dollars per share by the stock price, and expressing the result as a percent.

The facts are simple. Dividends are a major contribution to stockholders' wealth, in fact since 1926 dividends accounted for nearly half of the market's total return. It's also been shown that holding stocks in companies where the dividend increases each year results in a much higher overall return on average. In the last 40 years you would have earned 2 1/2 times more money on your investments holding stocks with increasing dividends compared with stocks which have a fixed dividend.

That said, one of the elements of this much greater growth is because of reinvesting dividends, and if you do not need the income then this is certainly the way your account should be set up. Taking Coca-Cola as an example, a share cost $40 in 1919 when it went public. If you had bought one share it would now be worth nearly $400,000 after taking share splits into account, or approximately 1,000,000% increase over nearly a century, which is not bad. If you had chosen instead to reinvest the dividends paid over the years, your $40 share would now be worth about $11 million, which I think you would agree is much better.

Looking for Growth

The growth investor is looking for a company that is expected to increase its business year on year. Good examples of this would be companies that are developing new products in an industry that experiences progressive changes and developments, such as for example some of the technology areas.

Growth is a measurement of earnings and/or sales over a period of time, often over the past year. You simply express growth by dividing the increase in a financial figure by the same financial figure at the start of the period, and multiplying by 100 to make it a percentage.

You may remember that one of the basic indicators of a company is the P/E ratio. That is the share price compared with the earnings per share. But you can also look at earnings per share growth to evaluate the company's rate of growth.

The summary page for IBM gives an earnings per share (EPS) number directly, which in this case is 14.09. (The ttm after EPS in the summary simply means "trailing twelve months", i.e the basis for the number is the last twelve months' figures). It is calculated from the company's net income divided by the average number of shares. In this case there is no previous EPS number, so you cannot figure the growth from it. Instead you must look at the annual earnings numbers.

You might choose to measure growth from the Earnings Before Interest And Taxes given, which was $22,361 million in 2012 and $21,414 million in 2011. Working this out, there is an increase of $947 million from year to year so dividing this by $21,414 million you get 0.044, or 4.4% growth.

As with most things these days, you do not need to work this out as many websites will give you growth numbers based on a number of different parameters. Incidentally, a similar parameter to the one I used which is called Earnings Before Interest Taxes Depreciation and Amortization (EBIDTA). This is another measure of a company's performance that you may run across, and is liked because again it is more difficult for the accountants to hide numbers that are not favorable.

There are a number of different ways of looking at growth, all calculated in a similar way to the example above.

For instance, you can look at net income growth, which is derived from figures at the bottom of the income statement. For IBM this works out to 4.5% on the basis of the income statement numbers. Net income growth is not the same as sales growth, as sometimes companies are gearing up, taking on more staff, and spending money on advertising, all of which causes the growth in profits, the net income, to be less than revenue growth.

If on the other hand if a company is paring down, and applying cost savings the net income may grow more strongly than sales income. You need to take a view on what factors are influencing any differences.

While you might expect the EPS number to be similar to the net income growth, this is not always the case. If earnings growth is higher then that suggests that the company is using its spare money to buy back some shares, and if the net income is higher the company may be selling off additional shares into the public market.

And you can of course look at growth over more than a year, and other popular periods are three years, five years and seven years.

Finding a Value

Value investing is sometimes spoken about as if it is an alternative to growth investing. This is not strictly the case, as you will see. No less a person than Warren Buffett denied this idea by saying, "Growth and value investing are joined at the hip. Value is the discounted present value of an investment's future cash flow; growth is simply a calculation used to determine value."

The classic value investment would be a stock which is undervalued, and which you buy just before the price begins to take off. But any short term trader will tell you that it is difficult if not impossible to know when a price is about to surge. In practice, value investing might mean identifying an undervalued stock and buying it in the hope that other investors will come to realize its "true value" and start buying it, pushing the price up.

Some people say that value and momentum can be used together to advantage. In this case the value side looks for a P/E ratio which is less than the average for the sector, and the momentum side would look for shorter-term moving averages being above a 200 day moving average. Of course you still need to perform your other checks for risk, and for unusual circumstances affecting the figures.

Gaining From Splits

In the chapter about the workings of the stock market, I mentioned that companies sometimes decide to do a "stock split". This increases the number of stocks on the market while proportionately reducing the price so that the total company value remains the same. The example I gave was Warren Buffett's company, Berkshire Hathaway, which did a stock split in 2010, splitting each of its $3400 shares into 50 new shares, which then work out to be $68 each.

The advantage is that the shares are much more affordable, and this means that more people are likely to be interested in them. Usually companies do not wait until the value is so high. Quite often companies will split their shares two-for-one, giving each shareholder two new shares at half the price of the old one.

A stock split does not change the total value of the company on the stock market. However, if you think about it, the reason the company does a stock split is because the price of its shares has risen, and there is an expectation that the price will go up more – otherwise there would be little point in going through the motions.

Someone has of course analyzed this and found that if you invest in stocks when they have split, you are investing in shares which are likely to increase readily in value. Just as an example, here's a chart of the Berkshire Hathaway values since 2010: –

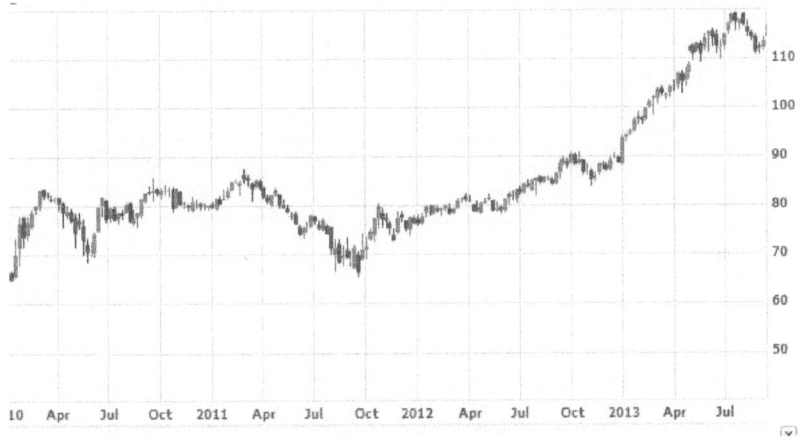

You can see that initially the price did not take off, but in three years it has risen to over 110, which for a split price of 68 means an increase of over 60%. The research on this method of finding stocks to invest in suggests that the optimum length of time to hold the stocks is 30 to 36 months, as this is when the maximum gains tend to occur.

If you're interested in this method of stock picking, then you can find more information by going to the website aptly named **www.2-for-1.com** which is run by Neil Macneale III.

Insider Buying

Another strategy that you will find with its advocates is "following the money", specifically researching when high-level employees are buying heavily into their own companies. You are not "insider trading" as you know nothing more than any other investor; but the fact that someone who may know more is confident enough to invest heavily in shares can give you a pointer.

It is relatively easy to find out the buying and selling by the management of the company as it must be recorded with the Securities And Exchange Commission (SEC). There are newsletters and websites set up based on the premise that such purchases are worth examining. One such website is **www.insiderinsights.com**, again not an affiliate link, which you can look at for more information.

When you're looking at the trades that those who may know more than you are making, you should be careful to differentiate buying and selling. There is little other reason to buy than you think the price is going to go up. On the other hand, people may sell shares at different times for a variety of reasons. Perhaps they are buying a new house, replacing a car, or just have unexpected bills. Selling shares does not mean necessarily that the price is expected by the insiders to go down.

So focus on published insider buying, and be careful to check out the company in other ways. After all, the CEO may simply have negotiated an option to buy a number of shares at a discount when he signed on. The fact that he takes up this option for an instant profit does not mean the shares are going to increase much more, although it is unlikely there are going to fall otherwise he wouldn't have exercised the option.

The Answer?

Given this information, it is now up to you to decide the level of risk and performance that you want to pursue, and the strategy that most appeals to you. To go further with your stock selection, you may need to use a "stock screener", which is software or a website that will allow you to enter parameters and weed out the companies that don't match up with your desires.

You can Google for "stock screener", and currently you'll get nearly 200,000,000 results. If you're a numbers person, you may like the Yahoo screener, which allows you to enter different values from drop-down boxes, see below: –

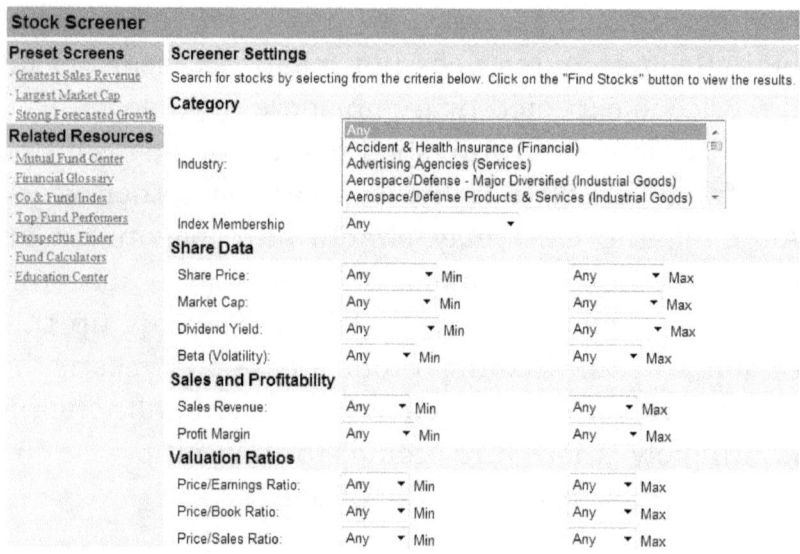

Note that there is more to this screener, this was a page grab from my monitor.

Another readily available alternative stock screener is the Google screener, which allows you to use sliders to adjust the main values: –

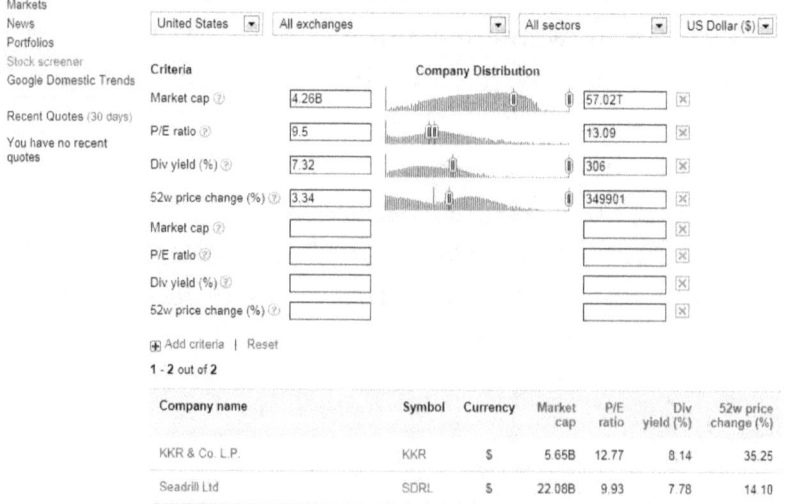

In either case, the screener allows you to choose the market sector that is analyzed, so you are able to easily keep your investments diversified.

As useful as these stock screeners are, I would still recommend that you take time to study the written accounts of any company that you are considering investing in. The stock screener simply reduces the many thousands on offer to a manageable level.

Now Practice

There is little doubt that you can spend a lot of time playing around with stock screeners, simply to come up with a shortlist of companies whose fundamentals you want to look into. But when you consider the number of stocks that are available, this is time well spent. Here is an example of how you would start.

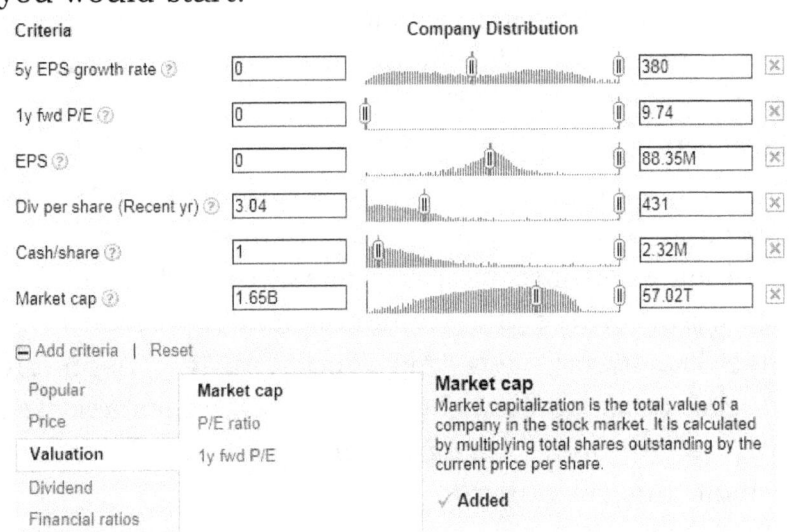

This is from the Google stock screener, and you'll see below the screen that you have the facility to add many different parameters – you can delete the ones already there by clicking on the "X" box to the right.

In this case the five-year earnings per share growth rate is set to be zero or greater, and the cash/share is set to a minimum of 1. We want the growth rate to be positive. Any parameters entered on this screen will be shown in the results, which is where the cash/share can be examined.

Next is the market cap which has been set to a minimum of $2 billion, which means only mid-cap and large-cap companies are being considered this time.

Last price will give us the share price in the table. The dividend yield in percent has been set to a minimum of three, so that the companies listed will all have a good dividend yield.

Finally the P/E ratio is included in the screen so that the information turns up in the table, though the screening parameters are not set.

In summary, this stock screen considers only mid-cap and large-cap companies where the earnings-per-share have increased over the last five years, and where the dividend yield is currently at least 3%. In my view this represents a reasonably low risk basic screen, though all companies selected with it should be further researched before considering investment.

Google automatically updates the results, and here are the first few from the screening parameters set: –

1 - 20 out of 160

Company name	Symbol	Currency	5y EPS growth rate	▼ Cash/share	Market cap	Last price	Div yield (%)	P/E ratio
CNOOC Limited (ADR)	CEO	$	14.13	48.95	93.27B	208.91	3.52	8.65
Icahn Enterprises LP	IEP	$	67.55	42.82	8.88B	79.05	6.37	20.27
United Overseas Bank Ltd (ADR)	UOVEY	$	4.70	32.81	26.65B	33.56	3.37	12.02
Bank of Montreal (USA)	BMO	$	8.59	29.61	47.88B	65.01	4.39	10.81
AvalonBay Communities Inc	AVB	$	0.52	23.89	16.90B	130.60	3.31	82.61
Sumitomo Mitsui Financial Grp. Inc. (ADR)	SMFG	$	-	19.63	65.39B	9.66	5.55	8.18
Siemens AG (ADR)	SI	$	7.61	19.54	98.86B	117.31	3.45	16.89
Thales SA (ADR)	THLEY	$	-	19.35	6.91B	34.65	3.30	-
Daimler AG (USA)	DDAIF	$	4.29	18.77	82.16B	76.86	3.87	9.23

First you will see that there are 160 results, which at least gives you a reasonable amount from which to choose while not being overwhelming. Some you may dismiss straightaway on further examination of the numbers. If none of these turned out okay after additional research, or if you had far fewer results, then you would have to ease one of the restrictions, such as reducing the dividend to 2.5%.

You can sort on any of the columns simply by clicking on the heading. In this case the cash/share has been sorted from large to small, and this shows that CNOOC has the most cash per share at $48.95, and the shares are selling at $208.91. The company name has "ADR" after it, and this stands for American Depositary Receipt – this is a way that American investors can trade in shares of foreign companies, where an American bank buys shares and issues certificates to US investors for them. It is a standard practice, and saves the complication of actually converting currency and buying the shares directly from another country.

By clicking on the name on the Google screen, you can find that this is a Chinese company, an investment company dealing with crude oil and natural gas, in other words in the energy sector.

From the point of view of looking for low risk, the most interesting company on this screen is the United Overseas Bank, also an ADR. That is because the cash/share is $32.81 and the share price is $33.56. That means that the company has almost enough money on hand to buy back its own shares, and this gives you a margin of safety.

Please note that I have not researched further into this company, so this cannot be considered a recommendation, but I am simply pointing out factors that you should be aware of and looking for. You need to perform your due diligence, examining the accounts, comparing the P/E ratio of 12.02 to the market sector to see if it represents good value, etc.

It is important to remember that you cannot lose by simply hanging onto your money, if no companies turn up that satisfy the parameters you are looking for. You should not settle for the least bad choice, but look for a company that is acceptable. Perhaps you need to change your parameters, or perhaps waiting a week or two will give you other opportunities, but no one is telling you that you need to spend your money straightaway.

How you go about this stock screening depends on what you are looking for. You may decide to choose your market sector first before performing the screen, and this will limit the number of results that you get but will allow you to diversify into the types of holdings that you select.

You may decide to only invest in companies where you understand their business, and where you think they have a commercial advantage over the competitors. The advantage should be something which is not easily replicated or delivered by others. You will have to do research to find out what the products are, as not all companies use their corporate name as obviously as IBM does, for example.

For instance, did you know that Kentucky Fried Chicken, Pizza Hut and Taco Bell are all divisions of Yum! Brands Inc (yes, really!). And Johnnie Walker Scotch whisky, Smirnoff vodka, Captain Morgan rum, Tanqueray gin and many other alcoholic products are made by the anonymous sounding Diageo plc?

At the end of the day, it is your choice, but speaking personally, I would rather put money into a business that I understood than invest in a company that is just a name to me.

How to Make Your Trades

Perhaps you are lucky, and have a relative or close friend you can trust who is a broker. But if you do not, you may feel totally lost when it comes to getting started in the stock market.

The good news is that you may not need to worry too much about your broker, if you make the decision to take control of your investments and not rely on someone else's advice. If you feel confident enough to be totally independent, then you can look to the large discount online brokers such as E*TRADE or Scottrade, and be fairly assured that you are not putting your money at risk, and not spending more than you need to on a share trading service.

If you would like to have a little handholding, then you need to do some more research in finding a broker. Provided you are prepared to do your research with independent resources you do not need to have a broker's advice, so your broker will be required simply to help you with the mechanics of buying and selling, plus miscellaneous information.

To find a broker who will give you the personal touch without taking you to the cleaners, you need to ask certain questions. For instance, the most basic question is whether the broker is registered, with what body, and for how long?

You can follow up this question with one that identifies the licenses and financial designations that the broker has qualified for. You can find these and other questions to ask your broker or investment advisor at the government website on this   link **http://www.sec.gov/investor/brokers.htm.**

While you are able to search on the Internet to see whether there have been any complaints against the broker you are considering, to be fair you must also check whether the complaints were upheld and substantiated, or simply the result of a customer who was dissatisfied for some other reason. However, there are many brokers vying for your business, so if there is any doubt you do not need to go with your first choice.

Account Operation

When you have selected a broker and decided to open an account, you will have to provide your personal details such as your tax ID or Social Security number as well as financial information. It is simple to set up an account and to start investing in shares.

When you tell your broker to buy or sell shares, you are giving him an "order". Whether you choose to use a broker who can assist you, or feel confident enough that you can do your share trading directly online, you need to familiarize yourself with certain terms used when placing orders. Not all brokers provide all the different types of order, but they should provide the most useful and most used types.

Market Order

The most basic order is called a "market order", and that tells your broker to buy or sell shares according to your instructions right away. The broker has a responsibility to do so at the best price he can, consistent with "executing the order" without delay. Your transaction will take place at whatever price the market dictates, which is usually the price you may see online on the broker's website, but could vary a little if the market is changing rapidly.

In the days when things were slower, you could expect to receive a stock certificate that verified your ownership of the shares in the mail. Nowadays, with the faster pace and online trading your purchase may simply be acknowledged by a recorded transaction on the screen which you can print out "for your records".

Limit Order

If you are at all concerned that the price may not be what you expect, you can instead try placing a "limit order". While the market order accepts the current market price, the limit order tells your broker that there is a limit to the price you want to pay, or the price you want to sell at. You're telling your broker that you do not want to spend more than a certain price per share, so do not buy the shares for you if the price is over that.

You can place the limit at the level you see on the screen, if you're just worried that the price might drift against you with a market order; or you could place your limits just below the current market price, thinking that regular price fluctuations will mean that sooner or later you will get the shares at the lower price.

Now if your broker cannot make that trade for you because the price does not move down, then there is a chance that you will never buy the shares. That is the risk you take with a limit order.

When you are selling shares, with a limit order you state the price that you must get for them, and your broker will not sell them for you unless the price is that much. Again, you could be left with no transaction taking place if the price never gets to your level.

Limit orders can be very useful to avoid any unforeseen problems. Certainly you have to consider that the order may not ever be "filled" by your broker, but if you are buying and selling shares that are very volatile, or do not trade in large volumes, then they can be invaluable.

Stop Order

The third type of order that is frequently used is called a "stop order". It is sometimes also called a "stop loss order", reflecting one of its main uses. In a way this is the opposite of the limit order, as it tells your broker to sell your shares only if the price goes against you – with a limit order you want the price to increase before the sale takes place.

The idea of the stop loss order is to close out your trade before you lose too much money. If you buy a stock and the price falls, then the stop loss order will instruct your broker to sell the shares if and when the price drops to the level you set. It helps stop you losing even more money as you would if the stock price continued to go down.

Because of the way it works, your shares may not be sold at the price you set for the stop order. When that price is hit by the market, the order becomes a market order to sell. This means your shares will definitely be sold, but does not guarantee the price you get if the market is moving rapidly. Occasionally this can be a problem, but often is not.

The stop order can also be used to buy shares. In this case you would set a level above the current price at which you want to buy the shares, and they would only be bought if the price went that high.

It sounds strange to commit to buying shares at a price higher than the current level, and you probably wouldn't use this method much. But in some strategies you may be looking for a price to increase before you expect that an uptrend is starting, and you're not interested in buying the shares unless there is an uptrend. That is when it would be a sensible and correct order to use.

Trailing Stop

A variation of the stop order offered by most brokers is the "trailing stop order". The ordinary stop order is when you set a level below the current price, so that if the price drops to that level the shares are sold and you don't risk losing any more money. The trailing stop order automatically varies the level of the stop order, depending on what the stock price does.

In use, you set the stop level a certain distance below the current price. If the price goes down, the stop is hit and the trade ended. If the price goes up, the stop level goes up with it, "trailing" behind it at the same distance.

The essence of the trailing stop is that the stop level never goes down. You can think of it as being on a ratchet. If the price falls down to meet it, then your trade is closed and the shares sold. If the price dips but does not reach the stop level, and then goes back up again, the stop level will go up, maintaining the same distance from the price.

You can see that this is a very handy way to ensure that if you have gains on the stock you do not need to go back and reset your stop order to make sure that you keep some of the money. If you simply leave your account until shares are sold automatically with a trailing stop order, then you will not sell at the highest price, but you will keep most of the gains that you made, without needing to intervene at all. Bearing in mind that it is almost impossible to guarantee you sell at the highest price (if you know a way to do it, please tell me!) this is a good solution to making the most of your investment.

When you buy shares, you will often place either a stop loss order or a trailing stop order at the same time, simply to protect your investment from a sudden dip. You should make sure that this order is canceled when it is no longer needed, particularly if you have the facility to sell shares short on your account. You do not want the stop order opening another opposite trade at some time in the future, just because you did not cancel it and the level was hit.

Stop Level

Some investors are relatively relaxed when it comes to setting a stop loss level, settling for an arbitrary 10% say. Others make more of a science of it. The perfect stop loss would exit your investment rapidly if the price was going down and would continue to fall, and never close out an investment that would turn around and make money. This is a difficult idea to encapsulate in a rule, which would only be right some of the time, given that the stock market is not wholly predictable.

One technical tool that I like for this is Bollinger Bands. When setting the amount of drift you want to allow from the peak price, it can help to refer to a price chart overlay called Bollinger Bands. These are available on the financial websites. The principle of Bollinger bands is that they are set at two times the "standard deviation" from the average. Here is a chart of IBM with the bands included:-

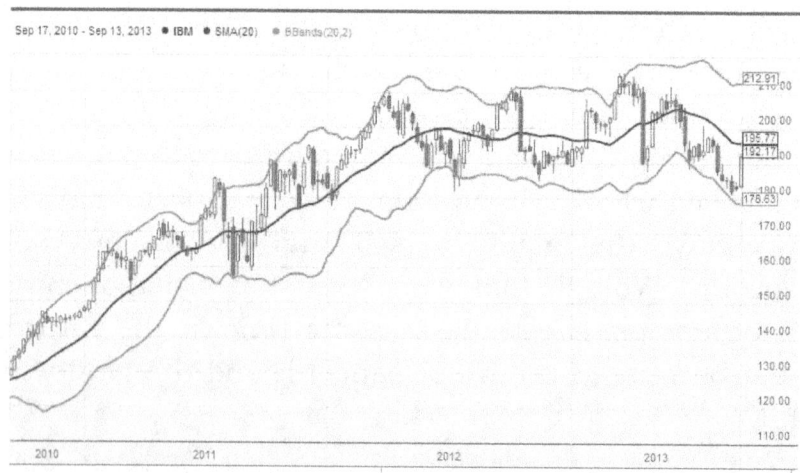

The middle line is a simple moving average and the lines above and below constitute the bands. Economists tell us that 95% of the time the price is expected to remain between the two bands, and you can see from the chart that this is probably correct. The banks take into account the price volatility at any time. If you set your stop loss a small margin outside the bands, then you are unlikely to be falsely stopped out of the trade.

You will see when you plot the Bollinger bands that they vary a lot in distance, reflecting changes in volatility of the stock. If you don't want to keep updating your stop loss distance, then at least you could use them as a guide for the general maximum deviation you can expect in the price.

Timing

There is usually a time element on the delayed orders that you give, and you can choose "good till canceled" (GTC) or "today only". These are self-explanatory, for example if you mark a limit order as today only, your broker will only execute it if he can do so on the day you place the order (or on the next trading day if you place the order while the market is closed). Otherwise the order will be forgotten.

There are a number of other variations on orders that you can give your broker, but generally they are used more for active traders, rather than simply to make investments.

Naked Put

Before leaving the topic of making your trades, I would be remiss if I did not talk to you about the use of the "naked put", which is a strategy using options. It can be used whenever you have identified a stock that you would like to invest in, but it is trading at too high a price at the moment.

Looking at the orders available to you in this case, you might choose to place a limit order, as many investors do, which tells your broker to buy the shares for you if they drop to a certain price. There is nothing wrong with doing this, and many people have been doing it for years to make sure that they "get in" at a price that would give them the best chance of making a profit.

However, a better way is to use options to enter the trade. This strategy is called the "naked put" as this describes in options jargon what you are doing.

For those not familiar with options, they are a financial tool that can be used to trade shares or many other "financial instruments", a term which covers many of the markets. If you spend money on an option, it will give you the right but not the obligation to buy shares or to sell shares at a defined price at a certain date in the future.

So if you buy a buying or "call" option, that means you can buy the shares at the price named in the option, even if the market price is more when the date comes around. With no obligation, if shares on the market are cheaper at the expiration date then you do not have to and will not "exercise the option" and buy the shares at the higher price. The price you paid for the option is lost, but that was the chance you took for the possibility of buying the shares below the market price.

If you buy a selling or "put" option then you have bought the right but not the obligation to sell shares at the price named in the option on a certain date. Once again, as the option buyer you only have to exercise the option if it is to your advantage. In this case if the market price of the shares is less than the option price, then you would choose to sell the shares using the option; if the market price is higher, then there would be no sense selling them for less using the option, and the option price is lost.

This is as far as many traders go in using options, but for every option bought there is someone selling the option, and collecting the money or "premium". Depending what strategy you are using, selling options can be risky. However, the naked put is not generally considered a risky strategy.

Before we go any further, you should note that every option contract is for 100 shares. The option price is quoted per share, so actually costs you 100 times what you see. Also, you will need to get approved by your broker to dabble in options. It should help if you tell your broker what strategy you are using, so he can assess the risk.

The naked put involves selling a put option, being the "option writer". The seller of an option receives the price or premium for the option, but has the obligation to fulfill the option if it is exercised, that is if the price finishes in the option buyer's favor.

So if you sell a put option, you must buy 100 shares at the option price if it is more than the market price when the option expires. That is the commitment you make as the option writer. But in this example you already wanted to buy the shares if you could get them at the "right price", and when you sell a put option you get to name the price that you will pay, and you receive a premium payment.

An example will explain the concept of the naked put. Going back to the ubiquitous IBM, here is a chart of the price over the last six months: –

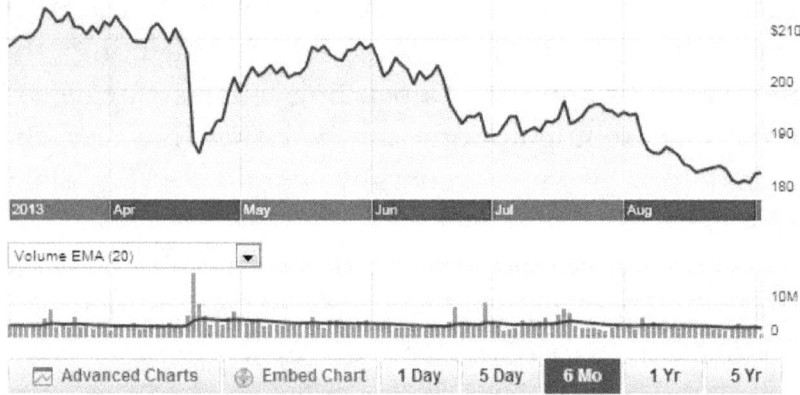

Suppose you have done your research and decided that you want to buy 200 shares in IBM, but you do not want to pay more than 180 for them. The regular answer might be to place a limit order with your broker, and if the shares fall to 180 then he will buy 200 shares for you. That would cost you 200 times $180, which is $36,000 plus commission.

If instead you used options, you could sell two put options and receive payment while you are waiting for the price to drop. Here is the option quote I just pulled from my broker: -

IBM

INTERNATIONAL
BUSINESS MACHINES
CORP

Price	**184.08**
Change	+0.12 (0.07%)

IBM 180.00 Sep 13 P

Price	**1.07**
Change	-0.16 (-13.01%)
Bid	1.06
Ask	1.08
Open	1.25
Volume	185

The expiration date is less than three weeks away, and 180 is the price just below the current price – these go in five dollar increments with options at this level of pricing.

Now what you could do is sell two options contracts, remembering that each covers 100 shares, and receive 200 times $1.06, or $212.

If at the expiration date the price has not fallen to 180, then the option is not exercised and you do not get any shares, which is the same as if you had placed a limit order. While you want to own the shares, the beauty of this system is that you are free to sell another put option as soon as this one expires, so you can keep receiving income as long as the price stays up.

If the price falls to 180 or below then you must buy the shares at 180, which is what you wanted in the first place. But what if the price drops below 180 – you still have to pay the full 180 to buy the shares, so aren't you losing out?

Not at all, as if the price drops below 180 and you have chosen the alternative of a limit order, your broker would buy the shares for you as soon as that level was reached. You finish up paying 180 anyway, and don't receive any premium while you are waiting.

When using this method, some traders like to take the premium received away from the price they will pay for the shares, so that they can see the net cost. In this case, if the price fell and the option was exercised the first time around, the effective price of each share would be 180-1.06, or $178.94. Obviously if you keep selling options and they are not exercised, your effective cost will keep falling.

You can find further details about options and strategies that can be used with them in "Options Trading – A Newbies Guide", a companion book in this Newbies series.

When to Sell and Move On

You can find a lot of information from many sources about what sort of shares you should buy when you are investing. What is not talked about so often is when to change your investments, or to sell your holding. As it is only when you sell your shares that any profit or loss becomes real, this is an important topic.

Stopped Out

The trailing stop loss is a useful tool, particularly if you do not intend spending your time checking on how your stocks are doing. As mentioned previously, if your shareholding is sold because a trailing stop is hit, you can guarantee that you did not sell at the peak of the market, the highest price. However, given that it is almost impossible to do so, the trailing stop is a very reasonable way of keeping most of your gains.

Stock prices go through cycles, and after a run up there is frequently a retracement or consolidation where you see as the price dipping down for a short spell before continuing upwards. Your temperament and attitude towards your investments will govern whether this concerns you.

If you were a short-term trader, you would certainly want to be out of the market while the price falls, buying in again once it is clear that the uptrend has resumed. As a long-term investor you may choose to be a little more hands-off than this, and providing the fundamentals are sound leave your trade in place secure in the expectation that the long-term trend is upward.

Only you can decide which type of strategy works for you. It is important that you think about this question, as it will govern how far away you place your trailing stop. With a trailing stop too close to the price, you may fall out of the trade with a small retracement which would be quickly forgotten in the ensuing uptrend. If you choose to set the trailing stop some distance away, your risk is that the trend may change into a downtrend, and you will lose more of your gains before the position is closed.

Buy-and-Hold

Some people say that "buy and hold" is a concept that no longer works. I can understand why they would assert that, but I think that there is no clear-cut case against buying a good quality company and keeping the shares for some years. You have only to look at the success of Warren Buffett and his company Berkshire Hathaway to see that buy and hold can work well if you choose the right companies.

That said, while many investors buy big company shares, such as Coca-Cola, McDonald's, etc. and hold them through thick and thin, relying on the long view, I believe you should keep your shareholding under regular review, at least taking an annual interest in the company's fundamentals, and preferably every quarter.

Fundamental Changes

Another time when you want to release your stockholding in a particular company is if its fundamentals change, and the reason you bought it in the first place no longer applies.

Say for example your investing strategy requires you to look for companies where the dividend is consistently increasing year on year. This is a fairly safe and common component of a strategy for selecting investments. Perhaps one year the company decides that it will not increase the dividends paid out. This could be because of financial restraints from a recession, because the company is undertaking expansion and needs to spend the money elsewhere, or several other reasons.

Whatever the reason, this is not now a company that you would choose to invest in using your strategies. Whether you immediately withdraw your funds to find an alternative investment, or you take a view on the reasons that the dividends were not increased, is up to you, but certainly you must place the company under review.

Similarly, if your strategy requires you to invest in the top two performing companies in a particular market sector, you may want to reconsider your stockholding if one of the companies slips to number three. Even though the company may still be doing very well, it is possible that your investment will be better served in the long run by switching.

Shifting Values

Diversification in your holdings is important, so you should undertake regular rebalancing of your portfolio. The companies that have performed the best will in time become predominant, and you will need to sell some of their shares and buy into the under-represented market sectors.

It is not in your interest to be too precise in rebalancing, as this would involve many trivial trades, but you might consider rebalancing if your holding in a market sector drifts more than say 5% away from its initial allocation.

Some might say that you are selling the shares that are performing well and buying more of those which have been disappointing, and question this practice. I prefer to think of it another way. By selling those that have performed well, you are locking in the gains; similarly, you would be buying the other stocks while they are relatively cheap. Remember that the market goes in cycles, and the disappointing sector may be the best performer next year.

Plan Your Investments

In previous chapters, I have touched on various ideas for your investments. Whatever way you approach your investments, there are some principles which you should keep in mind. It can help if you create a written strategy, and you will be able to check at intervals that it is working and that you are sticking with it.

Investing

As a principle, your investment funds should be used for investing and not speculating. If you are interested in trading in the stock market, in futures, or in Forex, then you have to recognize it for what it is, a marketplace where it is fairly easy to lose as well as win.

Certainly you can adopt a disciplined approach and better your odds of profit in short term trading, and I have written several books which advise on this. You must realize that commonly on these markets what one trader wins is another trader's loss, as rarely is real value added in the short term.

In contrast to this, an investment should be chosen to minimize the risk, and be made in something where it is expected that the true value will grow.

Limit Your Exposure

Even when you feel you have reduced your risk level, you should stick to a rule about how much money you put in a particular stock. A good number is no more than 20% of your total capital, and this assumes that you will be keeping yourself up to date with the progress of the investment, and not keeping it with the intrinsic danger of riding the value down if it turns against you.

Diversify

Following on from the above advice, I have already warned you about the dangers of investing heavily in one particular industry or market sector. Even though it may seem that you will not make top dollar, it is worth forgoing some potential profit for the security of avoiding an industry collapse, and using diversity in your investments. You can check out my book on Asset Allocation for further advice on this important aspect.

Use Stop Losses

Even if you keep a regular eye on your investments, it is a good idea to have some sort of stop loss order in place to avoid a catastrophe. If you choose to use a simple stop loss order, then you need to check regularly that it is updated in line with the growth in your investment; alternatively, you can use a trailing stop order that automatically updates. Be sure to use a rational method of placing the stop level so that you can keep most of your gains but also stay invested on minor price retracements.

Risk

The emphasis in this book has been on minimizing risk, given that the money you are investing is meant to be there when you need it, and not be gambled away.

An interesting idea is to partition your investment capital, keeping some in a core position that is likely to never to let you down, with other funds available for ventures that are more speculative. This is possible and can yield better results, but I would caution you against taking on too much risk, even with only part of your money. Always carry out your research and due diligence and know what you are getting into with the savings that you expect to be there when you need them, in retirement or for college.

Timing

The book opened with a caution about investing in the stock market if you need the funds at a set time just a few years away. The stock market is great for the long-term investor who can wait out the ups-and-downs. You should not be using it to deposit funds that you will require to pay for your kids' education in a few years, or to replace your car. You must be open to the long-term horizon, and then your returns will be good. If you know that funds are going to be needed in a few years then you should start pulling money out of the market in advance when the values are high, rather than waiting until the last few weeks or months and finding that the market has taken a temporary dip, carving a hole in your plans.

Finally, this book is specifically about investing in stocks and the stock market. Looking at diversification in a broader context, in my opinion you should not be putting all your funds into the stock market, but making money market, real estate, and other investments in a proportion appropriate to your time horizon. You can find more details about this on the website. We have seen in recent memory how the stock market can catch even experts unaware, decimating their funds. Do not let it happen to you!

Sources of Research

There are many investment newsletters, and you can use them for inspiration and to point you in the direction of promising stocks. With the information in this book, and continuing research, you will be able to evaluate for yourself whether the opportunities that they put forward are right for you. If you are interested in the performance of the various newsletters, I recommend checking out the Hulbert Financial Digest. This is not an investment newsletter, but a rating service that can show you which newsletters have consistently performed better than others.

If you are into financial matters, you possibly view CNBC and other channels that deal with the stock market. These are excellent references, but you must bear in mind that in the end, the commentators are only expressing their opinions and have no liability for your funds. The very fact that you can find commentators on the same program expressing different views should be evidence that you can listen but do not rely on their statements.

I would urge you to adopt the same caution when it comes to the Internet. Here are a few well-respected financial websites, and often they are trying to give unbiased and helpful advice. I use them for factual matters, such as the stock screening which works fairly well. Anything else is for you to accept or reject, so please do not believe everything that you read however well presented.

www.theStreet.com

www.Bloomberg.com

www.fool.com

www.finance.yahoo.com

That covers newsletters, the television, and Internet. Before all these sources became popular, we had newspapers to tell us how stocks and shares were performing. I still trust what the Financial Times puts out, again with the proviso that commentators may not represent your interests. The Wall Street Journal is also respected.

My hope is that with the details given in this book, you will take the initiative to control your own investments, and not rely on the advice of any financial "gurus". If you choose to follow any advice, make sure that you understand it, and that it is appropriate for you.

About the Author

Alan Northcott has been writing and educating in the financial sector for many years and now resides in Florida. His books have been featured on www.better-trades.com, and attract comments from venerable traders such as Greg Morris.

In addition to works published in his own name, Northcott has been responsible for the production of several trading courses, e-books and countless articles.

Other Books

In this series –

Forex – A Newbies' Guide

"For anyone who's even thought about Forex and didn't know where to start, I can't imagine any newbie Forex book being more helpful than this. The author doesn't talk down to you, and he uses analogies that convey the concepts quickly and completely.

And, I'm pretty sure that people who've dabbled in Forex will have some "ah-HA!" moments, because the essential concepts are so clearly explained (with great graphics) in this book.

For me, this book was an excellent purchase and well worth reading." – Aisling D'Art

Options Trading – A Newbies Guide

"Alan's Newbies Guide breaks down options trading to the newbie level in an easy to understand and follow style." – Usiere

Other titles by Northcott –

The Complete Guide to Investing in Short Term Trading

The Complete Guide to Using Candlestick Charting

The Complete Guide to Investing in Gold and Precious Metals

The Mutual Funds Book

The Hedge Funds Book

Asset Protection for Business Owners and High Income Earners

The Complete Guide to Investing in Derivatives

For full reviews, see book listings on www.amazon.com.

Final Note

For an individual self publishing, getting exposure in the market place in competition with the publishing big boys is one of the key challenges; but it is also one where you as a reader can help me enormously by spreading the word.

So, if you have enjoyed this book please help me to promote it, as well as other Newbies Guides to Finance.

There's a wide range of ways you can do so including:

- Recommending the book to your friends;
- Posting a review on Amazon or other book websites;
- Reviewing it on your blog;
- Tweeting about it and giving a link to the website or to my author site at **www.alannorthcott.com**;
- Posting a link on your Facebook page;
- Linking to my Facebook page or to my Linkedin profile;

- Following me on Twitter;
- Pinning it at Pinterest; or
- Anything else that you think of!

And if you would like to be kept in touch with each new book in the Newbies series, or if you have any other comments, please contact me at **alannorthcott@msn.com**.

Many thanks for your help – it's much appreciated.

Alan Northcott